A Cold Night in June

by

Sergeant Robert Lofthouse

Had you have known our boy, you would have loved him too.

Rudyard Kipling.

Dedicated to the British and Argentine families of those who fell on that dreadful night.

Mount Longdon, East Falkland, 11th-12th June 1982.

Foreword by Major Justin Featherstone MC

The Falklands Conflict was remarkable in many ways. It was the last British conflict over an issue of national sovereignty; the last significant British maritime military deployment; the last time that British troops marched for the duration of a campaign and the last time that a substantial British task force met a regular enemy without any meaningful air manoeuvrability. This was primarily a dismounted infantry campaign and its battles were fought and won in close combat in a manner that had changed little since the Second World War. In the three decades that have followed the conflict, the British military has seen a paradigm shift in the manner in which it operates as its most recent deployments have become characterised by their asymmetric nature and the rapid technological developments that have accompanied them.

However, one thing that has not altered over time lies at the very heart of British military capability, the British private soldier. The history of war is a human story, not one of purely dispositions, statistics and tactics in the abstraction. The characters within 5 Platoon.... are bound by the same sense of values, robustness, emotional intelligence and dogged tenacity that are so familiar to me having had the privilege to command such men in my time as an infantry officer. Their experience of war is one born of relationships and trust and the moral glue that binds them together, their non-commissioned officers.

As we accompany Archie and B Company of the 3rd Battalion The Parachute Regiment across the desolate and arduous terrain of the Falklands, Robert's treatment of the inner workings of such a force is both affecting and unerringly accurate. From the preparation of weapons, kit and shell scrapes to the orders given over a topological model constructed from earth, each episode drew me back to such moments when I was giving orders for battle, or chatting with my soldiers over a brew. It was such treasured moments of intimacy and familial interaction that have remained with me to this day. The sharing of hot drinks between Archie and Jamie may appear trite to the

2

uninitiated but this is the soldier's act of communion, a symbol of service to one another and central to the sharing of fears, anxieties, irritations and thoughts; conversations which are as essential as orders to the preparation for battle and, perhaps more importantly, for reflection when the last round has been fired. The honest exploration of these discussions is all the more genuine for its lack of artifice or caricature and its willingness to demonstrate the humanity of such men who shared a hot drink on the slopes of Mount Longdon.

Robert brings the detail of B Company to life and his representation of B Company commander and his Company Sergeant Major I found deeply affecting and humbling. Their relationship of mutual support and deep emotional integrity mirrors that of my relationship with my CSM, Dale Norman, when I was commanding my Company on combat operations in Southern Iraq. The small and constant acts of kindness and reassurance given by the.... CSM chimes with my experience and are framed as central to the moral integrity of the Company as it meets the enemy on the slopes of its objective.

When we join Archie as he enters the maelstrom of close combat, the ordered chaos, sensory overload and sense of unyielding commitment are both overwhelming and compelling. The author conveys the horror and sense of

3

movement without flinching but it is the extraordinary actions of each individual which have the greatest impact. My personal experiences of combat are relentless but distorted, almost cinematic images, with the single constant being the incredible acts of brave individuals who although facing the terrible reality of facing enemy fire were not prepared to let down the soldiers who surrounded them. It remains an irony to me that it takes such devastation for individuals to often show their greatest selflessness and humanity.

As the battle progresses and the cost to 5 Platoon and B Company mounts, the strength of the initiative given to the British junior ranks is made apparent. It is this thoroughly British concept of Mission Command that allows 3 Para the flexibility and momentum to push home the attack despite devastating losses. As each of the individuals within Archie's platoon constantly consider what they should do next, in the absence of regular orders, having lost many of their commanders, they are seen to act with authority and a savage pride that ultimately leads to the defeat of the Argentine position on that remote 600 foot high hill, despite the enemy's strength and the need to attack up the slope. Without this willingness of my soldiers to readily apply their initiative and often challenge my own thoughts, I know that my Company would have not have been half as effective when besieged by the enemy and would probably not have been as fortunate in its success as a result.

When the fierce battle of Mount Longdon finally succumbs to silence, we witness Archie's Company as they consolidate and conduct the wretched task of recovering the dead and wounded, before they march to Port Stanley, bloodied and exhausted, to await recovery by sea. Through his eyes we understand how important the need for a heightened humanity is at such times and how the need for a deep personal and shared reflection is pivotal to each individual's personal psychological recovery. The conclusion of the narrative arc places the act of sense-making at its heart and will be met with a greater understanding by many a former combatant.

In these pages, Robert has created a compassionate, emotive and compelling story that details the minutiae of a soldier at the heart of the Falklands experience. This is a lucid, empathetic and emotionally honest portrait from a ground-eye view of the British soldier in combat, clearly born from the author's personal experiences as a combat infantryman.... I remain honoured to have served in the field with many identifiable Archies and his authentic voice has remained with me long after I finished his story and that of 5 Platoon, B Company 3 Para and its desperate advance up the rock-strewn slopes of Mount Longdon.

THE TERRAIN

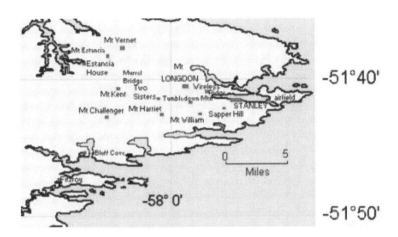

-51°40'

-51°50'

East Falkland: Mountains around Mount Longdon.

The summit of Mount Longdon.

After the battle.

Photographs courtesy of Imperial War Museums.

MENTION IN DESPATCHES

'A Cold Night in June' started out as a vivid dream, and the following people helped me make it a reality;

My lovely wife, Vicky, and my three beautiful children, who for eighteen months put up with grunts and one-word answers as I typed away, my two-finger typing providing my family with some amusement throughout.

Shaun & Nicky Langrish, family friends, who are the first official fans of my work.

Justin Featherstone, Matt Maer and Danny Mills, for giving me the time of day with regards to this project.

Dan & Natalia Henwood for their assistance with Argentine connections.

The Argentina Independent for their support regarding Argentine casualties during the battle.

Lawrence Ashbridge and James O'Connell, both Longdon veterans, for their best wishes.

The team at SDS Literary Agency, for without them, this book would not have seen the light of day.

CONTENTS

PROLOGUE: The Rocks

We got up mob-handed and dashed forward. Grabbing the gun by the carry handle, I legged it to the first cluster of rocks I could hide behind. Just as the light faded from one flare, another took its place, we were caught in the open and we had to get in amongst the rocks. Jamie was right on my tail as we slid in behind some decent cover. I tried to site the gun in a decent position with the legs down, but I was too exposed, as tracer smashed into our cover. Legs up, lower profile. As I tried to get into position, our rocks got hit with incoming fire. Jamie leaned out to his left and snapped off a few shots with his Self Loading Rifle, but then ducked back in, just as rounds smashed into our cover again.

Pinned down, another flare lit up our position. I could see all order of formation had gone out of the window. The guys were literally behind cover in various sized groups, just trying to get the upper hand. We had a fair idea which muzzle flash above us was giving us trouble, and some of the lads were giving it back, as I could see red tracer splashing all over their position. For a little while, the enemy position would be silent, but would start up again, maybe with a new gunner. The din around us was tremendous; machine gun fire, screaming, shouting, you name it.

I took my barrel bag off, as the strap was really chafing my neck. Jamie then grabbed my arm and pointed to the left. I could make out John shouting at me, but amongst the noise I couldn't make out what he wanted. It became apparent, when everyone dashed out of cover and took a leap forward. I quickly grabbed the gun, as Jamie had already begun sprinting ahead.

As I legged it after him, I noticed him jump over a small group of rocks. As I got closer to him, green and orange tracer began to thud and smash into the ground, just right of me. I went for the rocks. I then tripped, and got a face full of timber and peat as I fell to the floor. I was winded as I landed on the gun, my face killing me. I rolled over, and propped myself against a peat wall of sorts. The floor then started shouting Spanish at me, and as I scrambled for my weapon, it became more animated. A drifting flare above lit up what appeared to be a face. I fired, and this face shattered like an egg, showering the floor and me in brain, skull, teeth and blood. The gunfire rendered me deaf and my ears rang. Out of the darkness, another face and a pair of hands appeared and lunged at me, grabbing my throat and face. I grabbed at the wrists and attempted to prise them away.

"Jamie, Jamie," I screamed, muffled because my ears were still ringing. The guy engaging me was screaming

12

also. Didn't have a clue what he wanted, probably help, the same as me. "Jamie, Jamie, help me," I begged.

I managed to get my right boot into the guy's stomach area and pushed, whilst using my gloved hands to squeeze his wrists as hard as I could, which loosened his grasp. I managed to overpower him, and pin him to the floor. Still in control of his hands, I head-butted him again and again.

"You fuck, fuck you," I shouted, spitting in his face. He screamed out for help. I smashed my head into his face again. "Fuck you, you fucking fuck," I roared.

I ploughed my head into his bare face until he was silent. I let go of his wrists, and his arms flopped to the floor. I scrambled back against a wall of rocks. Soaked with sweat, I caught my breath, and in the drifting light of the flares searched for my weapon.

CHAPTER 1: Going Ashore

San Carlos. To the casual observer, San Carlos sounds like a lovely warm holiday resort in the Med, or if you fancy being more exotic with your imagination, South America.

Nothing could be further from the truth. The San Carlos in my life was bloody freezing, piss-wet through, and more like the Somme, just a shovel's depth beneath my feet. Our D-Day style landing was a far cry from what Hollywood had put onto the screen, and thank Christ it was not on a par with Omaha Beach either. We'd been sat on HMS Intrepid for days, and by this stage we had all had enough of being pitched and rolled all over the shop. When I joined the Parachute Regiment two years ago, it was all about being that warrior, launching out the door of a Hercules, and a swift and aggressive strike on an overwhelmed enemy. This was more of a Royal Marine gig, all this assault ship and landing craft caper. We were meant to get ashore in the middle of the night, but due to us not being accustomed to this type of entry into battle, and one of the boys breaking a leg going arse over tit with all of his kit on, we found ourselves crammed in like sardines, on this black and white crate of a thing they call a landing craft. In broad daylight, not good!

Stood up in the craft, I was sweating my tits off, the amount of shit we were given to carry in this assault was a joke! I had my helmet on, which to be fair was a lightweight design intended for Paras, and not them horrible looking frying-pan things the rest of the Army had to wear. We tended to fashion our helmet covers on our more revered airborne predecessors, the Fallshirmjager, German paratroopers. We admired their no-nonsense approach to soldiering. It was just a shame from a Para point of view, our helmets were not employed in a way they were most effective. I had scrim pulled tight over the top and a generous amount of black and nasty tape around the base to hold it in place, as for the rest of the Battalion, there were slight variations on the theme. Then there was my smock, a large, lightweight camouflaged jacket with built-in hood and large pockets. This in itself weighed a ton, with all sorts crammed in the pockets; clasp knife, chocolate, biscuits, notebook, pen, grenades, and head-over beret, which we took everywhere, a very crude olive-green woollen sleeve of sorts that went over your head, and acted as a scarf or balaclava. My lightweight windproof trousers were made of the same material as the smock, and included large pockets on the thigh area, which I made sure were empty, so should I have to start charging machine gun nests from the get-go, I could at least run to a fashion. The boots, well let's just say this is an item of clothing that the British Army had not really addressed in any real depth. They were crap! Ankle-high cheap leather, useless at keeping the water out, but fantastic at keeping it in. To make it even worse, we had puttees, proper Dad's Army kit, which we wrapped around the top of the boots, and after a short time in the field, they became just two sodden rags wrapped around your ankles. My webbing was a canvas construction that had a belt, a yoke which came over the shoulders of the wearer, and a series of pouches which had to accommodate other things you needed to fight the bad guys. My pouches had two lots of ammo and five water bottles. On top of everything, a canvas roll held my wet kit and warm kit. The other lads varied their webbing slightly, depending on their role in the Battalion.

The wet kit consisted of poor quality jacket and trouser combo that claimed to keep the water out. That was fine if you were static, but if you had to move about a bit, you sounded like a giant crisp packet, and you would sweat like a five-dollar whore. As for the warm kit, it was a jacket and trouser combo that was quilted, and up until now in my Army career, it did the job. It didn't keep me toasty, but kept the cold edge off me.

The final piece to my South Atlantic summer collection was my weapon, the General Purpose Machine Gun, known to all that have been involved with it as the Gimpy. This was a beast in itself, and just to remind me of the insatiable appetite this weapon had, there were 800 rounds of belt ammunition that had to accompany it. To keep it easy to manage, I had 100 rounds in the gun, wrapped around the body of it, the remainder wrapped around my shoulders and torso, giving me the Mexican bandit look, less the moustache, since bum fluff didn't qualify as facial hair. The more seasoned guys around me were displaying a serious amount of gringo 'tashes, which made them look even more sinister, when plastered in camouflage cream.

We carried ammo, grenades, bayonets, water, food, shovels, and some guys carried pickaxes and anything else that was of use in the assault. The powers that be felt it would be unwise to carry Bergen rucksacks ashore, which was good to hear, since that would have been more of a drama. We had enough kit to carry as it was. A Bergen is a large construction that you use to carry the remainder of your gear; sleeping bags, spare clothing, extra food and anything else you wish to bring with you. The plan was to recover the rucksacks from the beach once we had secured it, and we could then settle down in our positions for the night. How the rucksacks were going to get to the beach was anyone's guess, but I was just happy not to have to lug mine ashore.

17

We came ashore without incident, and to be fair, it was a mixture of both relief and disappointment. There was a bit of milling about on the shore, and then our section commander John shouted out. "2 Section. Grab your shit, let's go!"

He took the lead and led us off the beach, towards the high ground to the north of San Carlos, which was nothing more than a cluster of farm houses and fenced fields. Getting up there was a lick-out. We literally just slogged it out, up the hillside with speed being the priority, not so much tactical awareness. Once we got onto the high ground looking north, there was then the usual everyone trying to be in charge, siting our trenches and being moved around, again and again.

Finally, we stayed firm for longer than ten minutes and were then given the order to dig in. Our position was sited on a reverse slope, which to some would seem a bit pointless, and I must admit this was my first thought, but the method to the madness is that should the enemy see you at a distance, they can stand off and hammer you with their long-range weapons, but if they crest the hill then see you, they are already in range of your weapons.

The chance to get active was welcome, as the air was starting to chill me, since my outrageous sweat fest on the landing craft, and the Japanese death march up the hill. I was paired up with Jamie, who was my number two on the Gimpy. He would essentially be an ammo donkey for me, since he would be lugging another 800 rounds for my weapon, plus his own allocation of ammo for his Self Loading Rifle or SLR, which was a long, magazine-fed semi-automatic rifle of 7.62mm calibre. This rifle was a man-stopper on any given day, but due to its overall length could be a real pain in the arse when doing Fighting in Built-Up Areas (FIBUA).

Our section of B Company consisted of 8 men including me, 'Archie', and was commanded by John as Corporal. He had hard-as-woodpecker's lips, a no-nonsense operator who was part of the gringo 'tash gang. Covered in Para tattoos, he was the kind of guy you wouldn't want to meet in a dark alley. Despite his menacing profile, he was the ultimate family man, proud to be married with three young children; he was very old-school when it came to family values. He worked, his wife kept his house and children immaculate, and that was that. To be fair, after attending a barbecue or two in his garden, it was clear to see his family was his number one priority in life, but at work he was all about the regiment. Business is business, as he would put it. He was firm but fair with the guys in his section. He was the gaffer, and he wouldn't let any other

19

Corporals outside the section mess us about. There was a time and a place when you would get a bollocking if you fucked up, but if it was uncalled for, he would defend you, whatever the rank of the person trying to have a pop.

Our section second-in-command was Davo, a Lance Corporal in rank. He was a totally different type of guy to John; laid back, casual, but an awesome soldier all the same. Davo would not entertain good cop, bad cop, when it came to running 2 Section. John was the boss and Davo backed him in his decisions. That's how it worked in front of us, but off the radar, Davo would have a word with John now and again, should he have any reservations. Sometimes, John would U-turn on his decisions, this was rare however. Davo had no kids, but had a long term girlfriend, Sam, and to be fair, she was a proper tasty blonde; big tits, great body, and just lovely to chat to. She could handle herself, don't get me wrong. One night down the pub in Tidworth, Davo got jumped from behind whilst having a piss, and before we knew it had happened, Sam had battered his attackers, stiletto in each hand. You wouldn't want to be on the receiving end of her fury. I was sure he would make an honest woman of her one day.

Jamie was as mad as a box of frogs. He was one of them kids that had been left alone with the Coca-Cola too many times as a child. Face full of wholesome mischief, a smile

20

that would melt the heart of any girl that meets him. But don't let that give you the impression he was a soft touch. Our Jamie could handle himself, make no mistake. We joined together, and he was one of them bastards that makes everything to do with soldiering look easy. Our instructors in Aldershot had a Devil's-own job trying to wear him out, for he was as fit as a butcher's dog. He was due to go on his Fitness Instructor course before Maggie sounded the bugle to come down here and sort the Argies out, but he would get it cracked when we got back. Born in Germany, since his dad was a soldier serving there at the time, he grew up in Portsmouth, in the Leigh Park area of the city, which is as rough as any estate you care to find back home. He was always scrapping at school, but had the smile that would get him into and out of all sorts of trouble. Just before joining the Army, there were a series of visits to his home by angry fathers of pregnant daughters. They wanted to string the little bastard up, but Jamie's dad, always the mediator, would keep the wolf from Jamie's bedroom door. One evening, when Jamie was getting all tarted up to go out on the town, his dad pulled him up and sat him at the kitchen table, and read him the riot act, vowing that unless he got a grip of his shit, the next angry father would be led across the threshold and give him what he clearly needed. Jamie's cheeky smile and charm was not going to work on his dad, and Jamie did not have the bottle to call his dad's bluff. The next day he went down the Army Careers office, and signed up for the Parachute Regiment. Not quite what his dad had in mind with sorting his life out, but proud nonetheless. On 7th March 1980, I met that crazy fool Jamie - day one, week one at Depot Para, Browning Barracks, Aldershot, and you couldn't ask for a better mate. Just don't leave your sister or mother in the same room as him for too long.

The other guys in the section, Kyle, Zane, Brandon and Leighton, were the more senior guys, and had a lot of time under their belts. Having seen service in both Northern Ireland and Cyprus, they were also subscribers to the gringo club.

Kyle was from the South Coast, but was taken to Malta as a baby. Malta is not the biggest country in the world. In fact it's smaller than the Isle of Wight. As for entertainment for a bored teenager, you had either sunbathing and drinking, or fighting the surprisingly large Russian population. During the holiday season, Kyle volunteered as a lifeguard, and also had some form of medic training to keep him busy, but in the off-season, the island was a ghost town, and that is when he would end up drinking with friends, and it would usually end up in a brawl with drunken teenage Russians around a pool table or fruit machines. Kyle's folks sent him back to the UK to his grandparents for a while to sort himself out, since it was clear that he would probably end up getting stabbed fighting the Russian kids, since it was not uncommon for them to be tooled up. It was during his time back in the UK, he decided the Army would offer him a life that would hopefully bring with it some satisfaction, so in 1976 he joined up, and saw even more drunken brawling in his unit, since at the time the Battalion was serving in West Germany as part of a quick reaction force, driving about in Armoured Personnel Carriers, not quite what the paratrooper recruiting poster portrayed, but that's what their role was whilst out there. Waiting for the vast Russian hordes to come screaming across the north German plain got very boring, very quickly, and in hindsight, if the Russians ever fancied a shot at the title, they should have gone for it on payday, since by the time they came in sight of British troops, the British would have been too pissed to even give a toss.

Zane's upbringing was not the most glamorous of childhood adventures. He was youngest of two. His dad had an accident at work, so therefore was written off, and kept the home fires burning by bringing up the kids. Zane's mum had to step up and assume the role of breadwinner, and it was not uncommon for her to hold down two, maybe three jobs at once, just to keep bills paid, and Zane and his sister fed and clothed. Zane's school life was nothing much to shout about either; constantly in trouble, fighting on the way home, sometimes the odds were not in his favour, and his sister would have to help him out in a tight spot, when a gang would circle him like hyenas. This in turn would cause his academic school life to suffer; arguing with teachers, bunking off, giving his parents a load of stick, always getting kicked out of the house, and ending up at his grandparents' house, which was luckily just a few streets away. School was a lost cause on Zane, and one particular day when he felt a trip downtown was far more appealing than school, he walked past the Army Careers office. He rang the bell, and a rather overweight member of the Household Division answered. The recruiter let Zane in, and made him a cup of tea. The earliest Zane could join was sixteen, which was a few months off, and in any case, he would still need his parents' permission. The recruiter then pressed for which regiment he would like to join. Zane had to walk around the large office to look at all the different regiments on offer, in the form of posters. He liked the idea of being on tanks, but that meant a life sentence in Germany, not what he was after. He also looked at the Guards, but standing like a lemon, as he put it, outside some posh gaff was not for him either. He was about to sit back down, when he caught in his sightline a poster for the Parachute Regiment. Now this was more like it, jumping out of planes in the dead of night into the enemy's backyard, with extra jump pay too. Yes sir, Zane fell in love with the idea straightaway. The recruiter appeared rather relieved this scruffy toe-rag didn't ask for the Household Cavalry, and went to the filing cabinet to fetch all the relevant paperwork for entry into the Parachute Regiment. Once at home, Zane poured the pile of paperwork onto the kitchen table, announcing he was joining the Army. His parents were silent at first, then the silence was broken, his father stating that since he had trouble with doing as he was told at school, what made him think that the Army was going to put up with his shit either, more than likely the Army would knock it out of him. Zane shrugged his shoulders and asked for permission to join once he was sixteen, to which his parents merely looked at each other and shrugged, what's the worst that could happen? On his sixteenth birthday in 1974, his dad took him back to the Careers Office and signed the paperwork.

Brandon was somewhat of an unknown quantity, he pretty much kept himself to himself. He was a big fan of going home at the weekends, and didn't drink much, which for a Para was a very rare breed indeed. He didn't have any tattoos that I knew of, bearing in mind the rest of us were pretty much walking adverts for the Regiment. His view was that he was no less of a paratrooper, tattoos or not, fair point! When it came to birds, he didn't act like a dog on heat when he got straight back off exercise, like the rest of us. He just did his own thing, and maybe he had a bird back home. If he did, he didn't shout about it, and from what I can gather, he didn't have any kids. Just a very private guy. One night in the pub in Tidworth, one of the mortar lads came stumbling over, and accused Brandon point-blank of being queer. Don't get me wrong, I'm sure this guy was not the first to think it, but to blatantly poke the chest of the guy as you accuse him, you'd better have your facts straight. I almost choked on my beer when this happened, as we were all together, just getting a few beers in midweek, and before I could wipe my chin of beer, Brandon's head connected with this guy's nose, and the guy's face collapsed with the force of the head butt, his blood all over the shop, spraying all over Brandon's face. Our broken friend was now on his knees, using both hands to keep hold of his blood, and also muffling his own screams, but it wasn't muffled enough, as the barmaid let out a scream too. The remainder of the mortar lads came crashing through the bar towards us. No real time to prepare yourself for the ruck that was clearly imminent. I took a deep breath and just got ready to deal with my first customer. It was at this time John walked out of the bog, fag between his lips, doing up his flies, and the mortar lads offensive screeched to a halt. Both groups eyed each other, and then looked at John, whose eyes narrowed to a glare. He demanded to know what the problem was. One of the mortar lads informed him that Brandon had smashed their boy in the face. John then looked at Brandon, who very calmly said this lad poked him in the chest and called him a queer. John rolled his eyes and put his fag out in the nearest ashtray. He told the mortar boys to pick up their boy, to fuck off back to their side of the bar, and to behave, which they did without hesitation. John was one of the old guard, no one messed with them boys, he held a kudos all of his own. He didn't need a gang to beat his drum for him, he could do it himself. As for Brandon, nice guy, just don't call him a queer.

Leighton was another Army brat born in Germany. His dad had served with the Royal Hampshire Regiment whilst out there, but one time on a tour in Ireland, his armoured Land Rover got hit with a rocket-propelled grenade. This fucked up his hearing, and he was discharged on medical grounds. Now resettled in Havant, Leighton just had your run-of-the-mill upbringing; his folks used his dad's compensation to set up their own sandwich delivery firm, and also a cafe. Leighton was all set to inherit the empire his folks had built, but from a very early age had his heart set on joining the Army. He was Army barmy, bearing in mind he was brought up on the outskirts of a city closely connected with the Navy. His folks had no real reservations, but his dad wanted him to join a unit that offered a trade and life skills, since he didn't want his boy to go down the same road as him, and have to scratch himself a living once he left the forces. Leighton's granddad had been in the Royal Engineers, and was a boiler maker. Upon leaving the Army, he managed to land himself a boiler-making job in Portsmouth dockyard. Leighton wanted to travel and see action, and he was not going to find it making boilers. Leighton and his dad went down the Army Careers office, and Leighton asked for the Parachute Regiment. The recruiter asked why. Leighton said he saw news footage of them taking no shit in Northern Ireland, and wanted some of that. The recruiter raised an eyebrow at his dad, who just shrugged his shoulders, and the paperwork started from there.

So this was us, not much to write home about, but with us all sat together, heavily armed and with enough attitude to start a small war of our own, we resembled something out of a Sven Hassel novel. It was early afternoon of our first day at war, and so far, we got soaked getting from ship to shore. Then that long slog up the bastard hill to our positions. All we had to look forward to was an afternoon of landscape gardening, Army style. Digging in was our priority now, since an Argentine counterattack was predicted within our first 24 hours ashore. In the back of my mind, getting killed or wounded was not a concern, but how long were we going to be away for, a month or a year? The football World Cup was on soon and this pissed a lot of the boys off, and I'm sure there were a few Argentine soldiers moaning about why their masters wanted to invade during the World Cup as well.

CHAPTER 2: Digging In

Jamie with his pick, and me armed with a shovel, we started to carve ourselves a home in the hillside overlooking San Carlos Water. We'd removed the turf, and already we were sweating like lunatics, so we started to shed our gear, because we needed to be down and ready as soon as possible, should we need to defend the beachhead that was already growing by the minute. Stripped down to just shirt and trousers, I paused to admire the view. All over the hillsides surrounding the bay, there were hundreds of holes with troops milling about, trying to get themselves sorted. It was only later on did I find out that the unit digging in to the right of us across the bay were the Royal Marines. They'd had a bitch of a climb to their positions too, so our suffering was shared. On the water, it looked like a bloody marina, ships all over the place, to the point that it looked rather crowded. Helicopters with heavy under-slung loads buzzing from ship to shore, getting the beachhead established. Pallets of kit, ammo, rations, fuel, you name it, were already stacked up on the beach, very impressive.

"Fuck me, they're low," said Jamie. As I looked to him, he was pointing up the valley. As I turned, WHOOOSH BOOM! I dropped to my knees, ears ringing, and all I saw over the water were two shimmering orange glows going towards the ships in the bay. The glows passed through, and huge geysers of water shot up, straddling the ships directly underneath. My hearing returned. I could hear the cackle of automatic fire across the entire area. There was no one milling about their earthworks anymore, shit was going down, the enemy were here.

"Get in your fucking hole." I looked over to where the abuse came from, only to see John stood knee-deep in his own hole. He pointed at me, and then sharply to the floor. I dropped like a stone, not through fear of getting a direct hit on my trench, but if John had to come over and repeat himself, the only direct hit would be on my chin. Jamie had dragged the Gimpy in with him, and we scrambled to get smocks and helmets on. We then got ready to take on the next jets that came over. The theory is that you are to put a huge amount of rounds into the air, in the predicted path of the enemy aircraft. Fighter pilots are trained to fight other fighter pilots, and two chimps with a deckchair between them in a muddy hole is the least of their concerns.

John appeared on the edge of our rather shallow trench, which scared the shit out of us. "Right, listen up. A few things are going wrong here. Firstly, you are facing the wrong way. The ships are behind our position. Secondly, don't move anywhere, as to attract attention from these fuckers." He pointed up, indicating the enemy jets. "Also, don't waste ammo trying to get 'em, got it?" We nodded. "Sit tight and I will keep you updated."

He ran to Davo and Leighton's trench, off to our right. Facing the brow of the hill made sense, but the real show was on the bay. Me and Jamie took turns watching the show. The Navy was fighting for its life out on the water, throwing everything they had at the enemy jets. Huge geysers of water surrounded the ships, and the SS Canberra was sat slap bang in the middle, like a huge white turd on a snooker table. I didn't envy them one bit. These Argentine pilots were something else, they threw their machines around so low and fast, you couldn't help but admire their skill and bravery in equal measure. These guys were the racing drivers of the sky. Ayrton Senna in a fighter jet springs to mind; crazy, brave and dangerous. They seemed to go for the warships, not the Canberra. If only they knew troops were still aboard, it would be very grim for them. The Navy were starting to clock up the kills, now they had recovered from the initial shock of the attacks. One jet in particular came in real low, and appeared to just disintegrate in a hail of machinegun fire. What was left of the airframe hit the water and cart-wheeled below the surface. Scratch one racing driver, but the bastards kept coming, pummelling the ships, who with little room to manoeuvre, just had to sit there and scrap it out.

John came over to our trench again, this time at a more casual pace. "Keep digging. They are after the ships, in case you haven't noticed." We cracked on digging, totally unmolested, whilst the Navy was literally trying to stay afloat. We got our trench deeper, and so far no issue with water coming in, since the water table was so near the surface, even on the high ground. We had no overhead protection, just the turfs we'd removed at the start, but without timber to hold them up, they were no good at this stage.

The light started to fade, and the Argentine Air Force disappeared for the day, The Royal Navy was glad to hear. But the fliers would be back, no doubt about it. Looking at the ships, some of them had columns of smoke, coming from holes torn in their sides. One was clearly on fire, and this would continue into the night. I only hoped that all those onboard were OK, and casualties were light. At last light, John came back over to us. He said to take just weapons and mags in pockets, to the rear of the Company position, since our Bergens had arrived. I grabbed the Gimpy and some extra link, just in case. Jamie had his

SLR, as we made our way to the rear of the position, where we came across a line of tractors and large trailers. The residents of San Carlos settlement, who by the look of things lived like farmers, had offered their services to the Battalion, lugging all our heavy stores to where we needed them. Fantastic, great idea, don't get me wrong, but when you are trying to find your Bergen in the dark, amongst a pile of a hundred Bergens, it tests the sense of humour of the most hardy soldiers. We had guys cursing, some throwing gear about, some even giving up altogether, and leaving it 'til first light. After a long search, I entertained the idea, but Jamie said, "Fuck that, Archie. Put it this way. Keep warm looking for it now, and when you've found it, you know you're going to stay warm."

He had a point, keep searching. It paid off; we found our Bergens and made our way back to our position. Sleeping in the field, especially in a warlike scenario, is not camping by any stretch of the imagination. You have to sleep fully clothed, just in case the bad guys pay you a visit in the night, and you can jump out of your sleeping bag and start shooting. You can however concede a few items of clothing. I would take my boots off and put my trainers on, but I would keep my boots inside with me. Boots would go stiff or freeze if they were left outside, and if I had to get out in a hurry, I had footwear on to deal with any problems.

Besides, it was a small victory to get out of them horrible boots. I would also take my quilted suit off. You got cold very quickly, if you got out of your bag after spending the night with the suit on. Spreading your suit over you made life rather cosy, and when you got up, you felt the benefit straight away, when putting it on. These little charms of info made life as comfortable as possible. But there would be times in your career when you just had to grin and bear the weather, whatever you were wearing.

We got settled, but no sleep was to be had. The crazy events of the day were still racing through our minds. "You know what?" Jamie posed. "If their army is anything like their air force, we are gonna miss the World Cup." He had a point again. We'd have a scrap on our hands, if their soldiers were as crazy and brave as their pilots. It was not our turn on watch yet, so we arranged ourselves to face the ships in the bay. The wind picked up, began howling over the hillside, and I could just make out the sound of helicopters working like mad, to get resources ashore by first light. We lay there, looking over the water, paying particular attention to the ship that was still ablaze in the bay. We just chatted about nothing in particular, when there was a huge explosion on the burning ship. It was a few seconds later when the huge boom reached us, and the ship didn't seem to burn anymore. Jamie pulled the hood of his sleeping bag over his head.

"Rise and shine you pair of homos." I pulled open a rather frozen-stiff sleeping bag hood, to be greeted with the menacing grin of John, whose heavily cam-creamed face and outrageous gringo 'tash made it all the more of a wakeup call. "Danny and the Boss are doing the rounds this morning," said John. "Shit went down out to our front last night with Patrols Company and C Company, so they're going to brief us up on the facts. Get out of your pits and get your admin squared, understand?"

We both nodded, and he went on his way. We slowly emerged from our sleeping bags, like butterflies trying to shed their cocoons. It was fucking freezing. The early morning light was just starting to emerge over the horizon, the wind was howling like a banshee, and a frost had set in because it had been a clear night. I'd rather have cold, than wet and cold, any day. We got to our feet and straight away the cold hit us, so I dug into my sleeping bag, and felt for my quilted suit. Slipping it on was like a gift from the gods, and all around the Company position we could see guys doing the same, stamping their feet, even doing a bit of drill, just to get warmed up.

Admin, as John put it, was administration of your weapons, your kit and then you, in that order. There had to be a compromise on it though, because if an entire company stripped and cleaned their weapons at the same time, and the bad guys rocked up in front of us, things would not go well for us. The way we got around it was to work with your trench buddy. I stripped the Gimpy down to its basic working parts, removed any build-up of ice and frost and checked for rust, and cleaned everything with my gun cleaning kit from my Bergen, while my beautiful assistant put the kettle on and acted as chef. Once happy all was in order, and the beast was up and running, I applied a light coating of gun oil to all metal-bearing surfaces, before rebuilding the gun. Just to make sure the thing would work when we needed it most, I carried out a function test, to ensure the safety mechanism and firing mechanism would work when deliberately applied. To round things off, I inspected the 100-round belt, which had been attached to the gun for 24 hours. Once convinced the belt was free of rust and not kinked, I replaced it back in the weapon, job done. With the chore complete, I then assumed the duties of chef, so Jamie could administer his SLR.

Our rations were designed to feed the fighting man in constant action, and 24 hours-worth of food and supplements came to about 7000 calories. To the casual observer, this appears rather extreme, but average Joe in the street doesn't have to carry between 70 - 120lbs of weapons and equipment everywhere with him, and on top of that, have to fight with it on as well. The rations could support troops operating in an Arctic environment, where snow is in abundance, even though this wasn't the case in the Falklands; no snow, but loads of frost. To cook the rations, we had to supplement them with water from the bottles in our webbing. We needed to replace it from the local stream water around us. We were issued with sterilising tablets to make the stream water safe. Don't get me wrong, the stream water was almost black, and it tasted like you were drinking vile swimming pool water, once the tablets dissolved.

The ration packs were very basic fare. For breakfast, there was porridge of some description, and a mixture of sausage, bacon and beans. In a roadside cafe, this would sound quite appealing, but when you got it Army style, it had all the appeal of dog food. To wash the lovely feast down, we had hot chocolate mix, tea and coffee. Lunch consisted of a mixed selection of energy tablets, biscuits that a dog wouldn't even eat, and bars of chocolate that a child would ignore. And to wrap up, we had dinner, which was not too bad to be fair; pasta-based, or a type of stew mix. The rations did what it said on the tin; no thrills, bulk fuel. A real test of endurance for the soldier is having the same menu, day in and day out for weeks.

The next phase of our admin was shaving, and inspecting our feet. Being clean shaven has not won a war on its own, but soldiers with bad feet could well change the outcome of any campaign. You've only got to read articles from the First World War, to appreciate the need for decent footwear for fighting men, but it was still an ongoing issue, cheap mass-produced boots that clearly didn't have to be worn by the bean counters in Whitehall. Shaving for me and Jamie was a brief weekly flirtation with a razor, since we didn't really grow any hair, but the gringo gang had a real time of it in this cold harsh weather, when only a wet shave would do the job. My feet were in good shape, since I'd slept with my trainers on, so a quick change of socks, and back into the boots with minimum fuss.

Admin sorted, breakfast cleared away and Bergens repacked, we settled down to another day defending Queen and country. The sun was higher in the sky now, but it was no less cold. Jamie nudged my arm and pointed out to the bay. The ship that exploded in the night was still afloat, but in a bad way. She was very low in the water. The middle of her was as good as missing. The coal-black smoke of yesterday had now been replaced by a light-grey column drifting into the sky as if to mark her last stand, very sad. I felt for the Navy, stuck out on the bay. At least on land, on your own two feet, you had a say in the matter, more or less. She couldn't stay afloat much longer, surely. No more boats went to her aid, and she just sat there, waiting to die.

John was on his way over, with two other guys. As they got closer we saw it was Tony, the platoon commander, or Boss as we called him more informally, and Danny, our platoon sergeant. Danny was another one of the old guard; tough, no nonsense, and lifetime friend of John, I think they went through training together. As for the boss, he had a couple of years under his belt. In fact, I think he came to the Battalion the same time as me, but he had to go through Sandhurst, since he joined the Army as an officer, and if I'm honest, he was only about a year or so older than me and Jamie as well. As they got near our trench, we stood up to greet them straight away; Danny waved us to sit down. "Relax boys, just doing the rounds."

This put us at ease straight away. Back in Tidworth, you could either expect reward or a bollocking from Danny, especially if we'd pissed him off during the course of the week; fighting down town, not shaving before work, smashing up our accommodation during a drink-filled weekend, basically anything that would have him receive a bollocking from Dale, the Company Sergeant Major, who was the right-hand man of Justin, our Company commander. Straight away we could see there was a different issue to address here.

"Guys," Tony began, "just to keep you in the picture, Patrols Company was out to the north of us last night, recce-ing a possible site for a drop zone for both stores and troops, should our stay here be long-term." Patrols Company was the reconnaissance company for our Battalion, our early-warning eyes and ears essentially. "During the night, Patrols Company ambushed a platoon from C Company, who just so happened to be patrolling the same real estate."

Me and Jamie just looked down at the ground, shaking our heads. "How did this happen?" piped up John.

"C Company's patrol programme was not scrutinised before they went out," Tony explained. "If it was, they could have avoided Patrols, who were the primary call sign, out in front of our positions. A couple of C Company lads have been bashed up pretty bad. They will live, but their war is over, maybe even their careers." We couldn't believe it.

41

We'd only just got here, and we were shooting each other up, without any sign of enemy ground forces yet.

"Hey," Danny snapped us back to reality, "it happens, won't be the last time. Besides, let's deal with the task at hand. Are you guys OK, your feet OK?" We nodded. "Good. Right, we've gotta shoot." He pointed up at the sky. "We can't be out in the open for too long, know what I mean?" They began to move off to Davo and Leighton's trench. "How are you guys fixed for ammo?" called back Danny. "Did you get much off yesterday?"

Before we could answer, John waved his hand dismissively. "Told 'em not to bother, the fuckers are too fast." Danny nodded, and continued on with Tony. We started digging through our webbing for our brew kit.

Sometime later, Jamie piped up. "Hey, check that out." He was pointing into the bay again. The broken ship had finally given up the fight, her back broken. All that was pointing above the water line was her bow and stern, she had lost her fight for life. Off to our right, we heard the crackling of machinegun fire.

John and Danny jogged past our trenches, on their way back to theirs. "Round two," Danny shouted. Two jets screamed across the length of our Battalion frontage, and then banked left into the bay, in order to give the Navy another pasting. We sat tight with our brews, with the best ringside seats in the house, for what we thought would be a repeat of yesterday. How wrong we were. The Navy gunners had their shit squared for this round, and weren't going to get caught napping on this one. They were waiting for Ayrton and his mates. The Argentine pilots were no less crazy or brave than yesterday, but their efforts didn't come to much this time round, since we now had surface-to-air missiles, all set up on shore and on the gunnery rails of ships, and the gunners had got very deadly overnight. Ayrton and Co. were dropping like flies, and those that survived their runs were disappearing out of sight, with smoke trailing from their machines.

Where were the Harriers, we were meant to have? Little did I know that the pilots coming into the bay to attack our ships were in fact the survivors of some tasty dogfights with our Harriers, who intercepted them during their run from the Argentine mainland. I guess there were more of them than there were of us, so some were bound to slip through the net. By early afternoon, the attacks had all but faded away, as they had taken major losses during the morning. We couldn't get too cocky and start larking about outside our trenches, but the pressure was off, at least for the time being.

Our next trench visitor was Davo, all full of smiles as usual. As he rocked up, he started to chuckle. "Good to see your abortion of a trench looks as bad as mine." He had a point. Our trench looked more like a ragged shell hole, than a trench to NATO specifications. "Listen, pallets and timber and shit is getting brought up from the farm. You're gonna get a pallet and some timber to sort out your Over Head Protection. Go down to Dale's position, and he will give you your timber and pallet."

Nothing beat having a roof over your head, even if it was just a pallet with turf on it. So weapons and mags only, we trotted towards Dale's trench, which he shared with his Signaller Robin, who had the wonderful task of moving about with his Bergen all the time, since he had to man the radio set everywhere Dale went, what a treat. We were part of 5 Platoon, and we were dug in forward-right on the Company position, with 4 Platoon forward-left, so our Company had a two-platoon frontage in which to fight enemy ground forces, should they make an appearance. Just behind where both platoons linked up in the middle, was Justin's trench, which he shared with his Signaller and pack mule, Trevor. About 100 metres behind Justin was 6

Platoon, who would act as a reserve. They would basically bolster the main line, should us and 4 Platoon have trouble holding the enemy at bay. 6 Platoon would act as a counterattack force, deploying left or right of the main line to beat the enemy back, taking pressure off the two lead platoons, should the enemy not have its act together whilst trying to push through the main line. Dale's trench was just behind 6 Platoon, sited in such a position that he would be able to read the battle Platoons 4 and 5 were fighting. He would then be able to direct 6 Platoon to the best possible position. As we got to Dale's trench, we could see once again some of the tractors from yesterday, along with their huge trailers, off-loading pallets and timber to the small queue of customers forming at the rear. "Alright lads?" Dale winked.

"Yes sir," we replied.

He pulled out a flask from his trench and poured himself a brew. "Wanna sip?" We accepted his offer, and I tell you what, this tea was a gift from the gods, and was not ration tea at all.

"Where did you get this?" I asked.

He just winked at me, tapping his nose with his gloved hand. "Never you mind, Archie boy, never you mind. Besides, grab your pallet and get yourself sorted, them tossers might come back with ground troops on the menu."

We moved to the back of a trailer, and received our pallet and two planks of timber. A haggard old guy rambled away at us, and burst out laughing, which then turned into a hacking cough. We just smiled at him. We started lugging the timber and pallet back up to our trench. 6 Platoon were as good as finished with their trench upgrade, since them jammy bastards were nearest when the tractor arrived.

"Was that English the old boy said or what?" Jamie asked.

"Fuck knows," I shrugged. "It sounded either Cornish or South African to me."

Jamie adjusted the planks to a more comfortable position. "Whatever it was, it was proper fucked up." I grunted, getting the hump with the pallet already.

We wasted no time in getting our roof on, and very carefully placing on the turfs we'd put to one side from yesterday. We got inside, and had to make sure we could fight the position if we had to, with both the Gimpy and SLR pointing out a firing slit. It was a bit tight, but I suppose you have to just piss with the cock you've got. We walked out to the front of our position and admired it. It wasn't too bad. We ventured further away towards the crest of the hill and peered over the top, before committing our eyes to skyline. As the hill dropped slowly away on the other side, there were miles and miles of nothing, total bare-arsed open ground. "They're out there somewhere," I said, "and if they're not gonna come to us, then I guess it will be us going to pick a fight with them."

I looked at Jamie. He was looking back at our position. Dale was stood at the back of our trenches, talking with Danny. John was waving at us to get back to him, rapido. We jogged down off the skyline. The group was growing rapidly, since the entire platoon was now gathering around Dale.

"Shit is going down, mate," mumbled Jamie, as we reached the group. Everyone was taking a knee in front of Dale. "Listen up, guys. The Company commanding officer is away at orders right now, since things have all now changed, and we need to act now." He paused to allow it to sink in. "Brigade had planned for us to take several bounds west towards the main defensive area around Port

Stanley over the next couple of days, using Chinooks." Chinooks were large double-rotor helicopters that can lift heavy stores or almost a company of troops in one lift. "But earlier, a container ship called the Atlantic Conveyor was sunk in an air raid, with all but one of the Chinooks on board." Groans spread through the group. Dale raised a hand to keep order. "Brigade plan for us and the commandos to move west on foot, later today. More details will follow, so get yourselves squared for TABbing, and I will get more info to you as I find out more. Look sharp boys, this shit just got very real."

Back at our trench, we set about getting ready, for what was on the cards was a bloody long TAB. TAB in Army speak means Tactical Advance to Battle, carrying literally what you need to fight the enemy, and no luxuries. John came up to our trench. "No Bergens for this one. Be prepared to be away from them for at least 48 hours. Once you've packed your shit, get your Bergens stacked up behind 6 Platoon. Danny will be marking the platoons' Bergens, so make sure you put yours in the right pile." He trotted off to see Davo next door.

All weapons and ammo were to be taken; Gimpy, spare parts wallet, gun cleaning kit, spare barrel, two high-explosive grenades, two smoke grenades, one white

48

phosphorous grenade. The weapons and ammo weighed enough on its own, but then we had to make sure we had enough water and rations to sustain us. We rammed many of the set meals we had in our Bergens into our webbing. The chocolate, biscuits and sweets went into our smock pockets.

Then came clothing for the march. I was already wearing a shirt, green Army woollen jersey, a quilted jacket and my smock, but I would be stripping down to just shirt and smock for the march, since I would be soaked in sweat within a mile. So the quilted gear went back into the canvas roll along with my waterproofs. My jersey and poncho sheet would be going in the barrel bag, that us gunners got to lug as well. My poncho consisted of a large sheet of waterproof material, not too dissimilar to the waterproofs issued to us, but it had a drawstring hood in the middle, so it too could be a waterproof jacket of sorts, but also had ringed eyelets at the corners, so with small tent pegs and elasticated hook bungees, which you see in various colours when you go camping, you could alternatively erect a temporary shelter. It wouldn't keep you warm, but should keep the wind and rain off you. Last to be found a home were three pairs of socks; one set in my inside pocket, the remaining two sets in the barrel bag.

Not happy that my trainers and sleeping bag were going to be left in the Bergen for now, I shouldered it, and set off down to the rear of the Company position to drop it off. There were troops everywhere, sorting Bergen piles out for each platoon, grabbing last-minute bits and pieces from them, or stuffing gear into them that the owner felt he didn't need, or didn't want to carry. I found our platoon pile, and put mine down next to it.

"The locals are going to pull all our heavy gear for us in their trailers," Danny commented. "Bloody nice of 'em, don't you think?" I just nodded and smiled. Further down the hill, towards where Battalion Headquarters were located, I could see a lot of our heavy weapons and their ammo being loaded onto tractor trailers, since the Fire Support Company guys would be TABbing also, but without their monstrous loads, such as their mortars, anti-tank weapons and heavy .30 Cal machineguns. As I was making my way back up to my position, John had already got the section into a huddle, so I got a jog on, expecting a bollocking for being late.

He looked round to me. "Archie, park your arse there." I knelt down next to Brandon, who just winked at me, offering me a sip of his brew. "Right guys," continued John, "in a minute, we are going to start TABbing west towards a place called Teal Inlet, about 40 kilometres away." Someone gave out a low whistle. "Patrols will be leading, so they can give the Battalion advance warning of any trouble we may encounter on the route. The ground we will be covering will be hard going, so watch where you place your footing, don't want anyone busting an ankle. The commanding officer intends for us to rest for five in every hour. The pace won't be outrageous, but with all our gear and the terrain, it won't be a stroll either. Order of march; 6 Platoon will lead followed by Company HQ, then 5 Platoon, finally 4 Platoon. Don't collapse your trenches. They will be occupied by follow-on troops, fuck knows who. But leave them as they are. Once you've got your gear on, just sit in front of your trenches, so I can see that you are ready. Any questions?"

There were none. I think we were all just getting our minds ready for a bloody long night. Me and Jamie got our kit on and took the time to ensure it was going to be as comfortable as possible for the night ahead. I took my green woollen jersey off in preparation for the march, and for a brief period took a look at the parachute wings sewn on the upper right arm. If you had completed the Basic Parachute Course at RAF Brize Norton, you earned the right to wear your wings on the upper-right arm of all your military clothing, with the exception of your fitness gear.

"Well, Archie boy," I said to myself, "this is one of them times where you need to be careful of what you wish for." You busted a gut in training to wear those babies, and become a fully paid-up member of the Parachute Regiment. And this was what you got, the kudos of being a paratrooper, but the harsh tough missions that are part of the job description for a tough unit. Truth be known, that also went for the commandos dug in across the bay. They had a somewhat longer history than us, but they all carried the kudos of being a commando, and what came with it. Both the commandos and us had a long professional rivalry, and don't tell anyone I said this; they are a good tough bunch of operators.

Jersey stowed in my barrel bag, I refitted my smock, ensuring all the pockets were done up, and the right kit was stowed for easy access. Notebook and pen, field dressing. Morphine, which was issued prior to the landings, so should we have a casualty, you gave the casualty his morphine, and not your own. Biscuits, chocolate and sweets, which I could shove in my gob on the move. Socks, beret, clasp knife, smoke grenade.

On went my webbing, fully packed out with the rest of my fighting gear. On top of that, 600 rounds of belt ammunition for the Gimpy. I was sporting the Mexican bandit look for this march, with 100 on the gun, and the remaining 100 crammed into the barrel bag, which was the next item to go on. I could already feel the strain on one's legs without even taking a step yet. I pulled the straps tighter and jumped up and down to make sure nothing was going to rattle or fall off. Once happy, I then slumped on the ground next to Jamie, who was already kitted up and was slowly putting fresh cam cream onto his face. I positioned myself next to him, with the gun and my helmet alongside, and I then began to apply fresh cam cream also. Once complete, we just looked out onto the bay and the surrounding hillsides, watching other units getting their shit sorted for the move west.

It was about mid-afternoon now, and we would start to lose light shortly. Looking left and right of me, I could see the other lads in the Company, sat outside their trenches, putting on fresh cam cream, smoking, picking their noses, scratching their balls, some just put their heads back onto their gear and got in a kip. The order to move out would come soon enough. John moved up and down the Section line in just his smock, carrying his rifle, informing us that Patrols had already set off from Battalion HQ, and once they began to establish the route west, C Company would then follow, then us, then Fire Support with the tractors full of their gear, then A Company. The Bergens would follow at some point, when the Company Quartermaster

Sergeant could get forward to Teal Inlet. Phil was a Colour Sergeant in rank. He was a nice guy, very can do, along with his staff, whose job it was to ensure B Company got bombs, bullets, food and water on a regular basis. He could also pull a few strings and acquire some little luxuries, depending where we were, such as cans of pop or bags of crisps, even bread. These little things go a long way for a soldier living on the bare basics. A good Quartermaster Sergeant is a bit of an Arthur Daley, wheeling and dealing, but never at the expense of the men he had to sustain in the field.

Speaking of logistics, down by the water's edge, I was completely blown away by the sheer volume of supplies that was piling up for us to fight this campaign; I'd never seen stores in this volume ever in my career. Pallets and pallets of ammunition, more than I cared to count, grenades, mortars, missiles, rations, medicine, were but just a few of the items stockpiled down there, helicopters still working like angry bees, getting the pollen from the ships to the shore as quick as possible. I'm no pilot by any stretch, but I'm sure the flying-hours rule had been thrown out of the window long ago, they were just going for it nonstop. Why Ayrton and his gang never spotted this pile of gear is anyone's guess. Just think, one well-placed bomb or gun run could have ended our land campaign right there on the beach, crazy!

CHAPTER 3: Moving Out

"Prepare to move!" Danny yelled, so that the entire platoon could hear him. To be honest, I welcomed this order, since having just a shirt on under my smock meant that the chilled air was starting to creep in. Jamie, being somewhat more agile than the fat Mexican next to him, managed to get to his feet before helping me up.

Once up, we quickly adjusted our kit so it was as comfortable as could be, since I'm sure the manufacturers hadn't designed it with these loads in mind. I then, with the aid of Jamie, half-knelt and half-squatted like a geriatric, and grabbed the carrying handle of the Gimpy. My helmet was hanging on the gun. I fitted the Gimpy across my midriff, the sling over my head and across my shoulder blades, which initially wasn't too bad an arrangement, since it evened out the load distributed across my frame. The helmet went on, and this Para was ready to go find the bad guys.

We started off downhill, which I found rather bizarre, since we had to climb out of San Carlos initially, but at the end of the day, I just followed the guy in front as we shook out into our order of march, everyone still a lot of stop-start. Ahead of us on the high ground opposite, the commandos were making their way downhill as well, towards our left where the valley came to a narrow apex. The ground underfoot was already showing the signs of surface water and bog, as we squelched almost ankle deep in it. Before I knew it, my feet were soaked, great! The TAB out of San Carlos was already having me get a sweat on, as my back and neck were starting to get wet with exertion. Our Company formed two columns as we made our way out of the bay. The commandos opposite us on the other side of a river had done the same, but then I noticed they had Bergens, the whole lot. I wasn't sure if that was a good or bad move, since we would cover ground quicker than them, even though they had sleeping bags to climb into, should they stop for a while. I also noticed that while we had helmets on, they wore their green berets, a good move in my book. I was starting to really get a sweat on under my helmet, and the bloody barrel bag was already getting on my tits. I adjusted the Gimpy to take pressure off my back, and then I noticed up front, both paratrooper and commando Gimpy gunners had it over their shoulder, holding onto the butt group, the part of the weapon you put in the shoulder when firing. That was good enough for me, so I quickly joined the masses, and it did make movement easier, since I could now swing my left arm in order to propel myself forward. Someone up front went arse over tit into the bog, and some of the lads let out a cheer, but the lad in question just swore like a man possessed, as a couple of the guys pulled him to his feet. I did not want to fall over, entertaining as it may be to my mates. As we started to climb, I was in full sweaty-mess TAB mode, but at least I was warm through the exercise. I wasn't looking forward to the night ahead, not because of what we had to do, but it was looking like it was going to be a clear night, and that meant only one thing - cold.

The going started to level out, as we got out of the valley. We continued to follow the river on our right, and the commandos were doing the same on the other side. Their pace was much slower than ours, probably due to their loads, but maybe their bosses didn't want to kill them before they encountered the enemy. Our lot however had a rocket up their arses, and really set a lick of a pace. It wouldn't have surprised me if the guys leading were having a pissing competition with the commandos up front, but I wasn't in the mood for any of that shit, I was more worried about turning an ankle, or falling face first into the bog that seeped out from the river, left and right of it. All of a sudden the pace slowed to a crawl, and the word came down the line to take five. We were stood ankle deep in a waterlogged bog, so the most I could do at this stage was take the gun off my shoulder, rest the butt group on a semi-dry tuft of grass, and lean with both hands on the end of the barrel. The commandos did the same; we were close enough to them to exchange glances and gestures. The Marine opposite me, who was leaning on his Gimpy in the same fashion, looked at me and shook his head. "Whose idea was this?"

I wasn't sure if he was on about the march, or his boss's decision to carry Bergens. "Mate, proper lick out," I replied. He grinned and adjusted a strap, before he stood up straight. We then got the order to get ready to move, and already the commandos started to shuffle forward again. We started to move again, pretty steady at first, but before long the pace got stupid again. Following the river is easy on the navigation, don't get me wrong, but at certain points it almost doubled back on itself, and the kit was becoming a pain in the arse. That 40 kilometres they stated was probably in a straight line. At this rate, we would probably clock up about 60, by the time we got to Teal Inlet. We got to a prominent right-turn in the river course, and I noticed that our Battalion then led off in an almost straight pair of lines, out into open country, whilst the commandos got wet crossing the river, and headed off north. What the fuck! Whoever makes the plans clearly don't look at many maps, I'm sure. I was to find out later that these commandos were heading to a settlement called Douglas, about 14 kilometres from their river crossing. Their job was to deal with any enemy in that area, then move around to Teal

Inlet, our objective. Apparently this was the plan all along, but with Chinooks instead. The plan stayed the same, but it would be done in the ankle-high, soaking wet leather personnel carriers, our boots.

The Marine I exchanged words with had his freezing cold foot spa for the day, as he passed in front of me. "All the best, mate," he said. "Last one to the bar in Stanley."

I winked at him. "Take care, mate, I will save you my trench in Teal."

The Battalion headed west-northwest. The ground started to get drier and more firm underfoot, and then the clowns up front started to hug the low ground, being all tactical and shit. And where there is low ground, there is water. About half an hour after we left our commando friends at the river crossing, word came down the line to take 30 and get a brew and scoff on. Me and Jamie found a raised bank of sorts and slumped against it. I was piss-wet through with sweat, and to be honest, I couldn't be arsed to get all the gear off, but Jamie, being as agile as a cat, was out of his gear and had deployed his brew kit and scoff, then the water was on the go. I shouldn't have been such a lazy shit, but all I wanted was to sort my socks out. I had plenty of grub to stuff my face with in my smock. Jamie scrambled around behind me. "Lean forward, I'll get you a scoff out."

I did as he asked, and he rifled through my webbing, and found me some goulash and hardtack biscuits. I then leant back as he continued to play chef. The light was fading and the cold was starting to set into our chilled bodies, so before I went completely into crow mode, I lifted my right boot, undid the laces and slipped it off, and pulled a rather wet sock off. Crow mode was a condition of idleness, where you had all the demeanour of a new recruit, a crow. I inspected my foot. It was all pruned, like I'd been in the bath too long. I wrung my sock out and placed it back on, then re-fitted my boot. The act of wringing my sock out made life feel a lot more comfortable, so I repeated the process with my left foot.

Once my foot care was complete, dinner was served. I tore open the bag of goulash carefully, not to spill any of the hot sauce on my smock. Taking my pack of biscuits, I crushed them up and sprinkled them into the goulash, which basically doubled the size of the meal. In my inside pocket, my spoon was stashed next to my spare socks. I had robbed the spoon from the galley of the Canberra. I tucked in, thanking Jamie for sorting out his fat lazy arsehole of a friend. He winked as he ploughed through his scoff. Not too sure what he had, it wasn't around long enough to be inspected. Food done, we savoured our rest time, and shared hot chocolate he prepared. He would make someone a fine wife someday.

When word came down the line to get on our feet, I was glad, due to the fact it was really getting cold now, since there wasn't a cloud in the sky, and at this twilight stage of dark setting in, the sky was just crammed with stars, and you could see your own breath in the cold air.

Once on our feet, we quickly adjusted ourselves, and our column started to shuffle off. I quickly settled the Gimpy on my right shoulder. Looking at the guys in the column up ahead reminded me of the footage and photos of German troops, advancing towards the Volga in the vast expanse of Russia. The cold that engulfed us just added to the atmosphere of this image I had in my head, of the Eastern Front all them years ago. The pace started to really open up now, and earlier I thought it was the pacesetters trying to prove a point to the commandos. Sweat soon made a comeback under the weight of my kit and the pace of the march. The terrain didn't help much either. It reminded me of Sennybridge, where we conducted most of our exercises back home; open moorland, hardly ever flat, and rough tussocks of grass that if caught wrong could turn an ankle, even trip you over. Water was present on the surface also, so it wasn't long before my feet were soaked once again. I wasn't sure if we were smashing the route out on a straight compass bearing to Teal, or those leading our column just didn't care for the guys who were really feeling it with all their kit on. We went up and down these short but harsh gradients, instead of skirting around them. There was no compromise, the pace was a lick. On the high ground, there were the harsh babies-heads, what the Army would call the tussock grass, and on the low ground, you had to slog your way through bog and surface water.

After what seemed like hours, we stopped for a breather. Soaked in sweat, I slumped to the floor and fished out a water bottle. Despite the cold night, the water in my bottle was refreshing, since I was finding the TAB hard work. I wasn't alone. Guys who were known for their TABbing prowess were feeling the pace. Big gaps had started to appear in the line, where guys started to flag under their loads. A few guys had fallen out of the march some distance back, probably due to ankle injuries, or maybe even exhausted, but no one stuck around to even see if they were OK. I just hoped the Battalion medics were dealing with them, and the casualties were getting put into the trailers being pulled by the locals. It was now getting really cold, even more so as my sweat started to get cold and dry. I pulled out my black leather gloves and slipped them on. They gave me some instant relief, as it got my hands out of the increasingly biting wind that had picked up. I stuffed some chocolate into my mouth that I had fetched from my smock pocket. I leant over and nudged Jamie, and offered him the rest of it.

He nodded. "Cheers mucker. I'm chinned, and this is a lick out."

I grinned at him. "Hopefully, there are no bad guys at Teal, and we can get some kip instead."

He chuckled, despite the fact that enemy forces being at our destination could be a very real prospect. If anyone was going to encounter an enemy presence at Teal, it would be the Patrols Company lads. They were ahead of the main bulk of the Battalion on this march, both proving the route to Teal, and also hopefully giving us advance warning of any enemy they encountered on the route, or at our destination. The Patrols lads would initially keep a low profile and assess what strength the enemy were, and what type of weapons they had, stuff like that. They wouldn't kick things off straight away, unless it was an opportunity too good to miss. For example, if all the bad guys were in bed or something like that, they would report over the radio to the CO, the Commanding Officer of our Battalion, Charlie. Charlie would receive the information from Patrols, and if he still had reservations, he would make us sit tight, and then go forward to see the bad guys for himself. He would come up with a plan and dish it out to the companies, who would do the fighting. Patrols would keep eyes on during the planning phase, drip-feeding information to the companies, so the companies had up-to-date information in real time.

 We ended up sitting on that windswept, freezing cold hillside for some time, and I was tempted to change into my warm kit, but me being the lucky guy I was, as soon as I got all comfy, we would be off again. I carried out a damage assessment of my aching cold wet frame. My shoulders ached from the Gimpy. During the course of the night, I had been changing which shoulder would carry the gun. My hips had started to get sore, since my sweat had soaked through my shirt and smock, and had now soaked into the canvas belt of my webbing. When wet, the canvas shrunk and got very stiff, so after a while the rubbing would create sores, which would make the march all the more unpleasant. I had started to get sweat-rash between my thighs, where they had been rubbing for the last couple of hours, and the fact that my boxer shorts were now a new design of thong, and royally rammed up the crack of my arse, didn't make the situation any better. My feet were not feeling the love much either, pretty much soaked since we last set off, and my toes and heels were starting to get sore, marching over this bloody terrain. In summary, all was not well at Chez Archie.

We started to shiver, resultant from being stationary for too long. A lot of the lads in our column had got their warm kit out, and just put it over the top of all they were wearing, to minimise pratting around. Enough was enough, and me and Jamie followed suit. It felt so nice. Why we hadn't done it earlier was anyone's guess. Looking left and right of me, I could see some of the lads having a crafty fag inside their quilted jackets, to cut down on the glare of their cigarettes. You could tell who was taking a drag and when, because the inside of their jackets would glow bright. If anything, it gave them something to do, and maybe even took their mind off their discomfort.

Jamie nudged my arm, and pointed up the line. I could see a figure making his way towards us. The smokers quickly put out their fags, through fear of a bollocking. As the figure got closer, we recognised the shape as Tony, our platoon commander. "Jamie, go fetch Danny, please," he asked quietly and rather politely.

"Roger that." Jamie shuffled off to the rear of our platoon, where you would find the platoon sergeant following up, giving those who were flagging a fatherly kick up the arse. John arrived with Davo.

"What's going down, Boss?" I asked.

"Hang on," Tony replied, "all will be revealed." Jamie arrived back with Danny, resuming his place in the column.

"Right guys," the Boss began, "we are about 16km short of Teal; patrols are pushing forward to get eyes on the settlement, to look for bad guys. This will take a while, since the CO wants no surprises when we get there, so you can bet your dollar on Patrols doing a CTR, before telling the old man we can go into town." CTR was Close Target Recce. Patrols would very slowly and very carefully push their way into Teal, crawling if need be, to see if there were any Argentine soldiers defending it. Patrols might even push their luck and peer through windows, to see if the enemy were sheltering from the cold. Nothing would be left to chance. Patrols would even sneak around and come in from a different direction, to establish whether the enemy was there. If Patrols found enemy, and the odds were in our favour, they would report back to the CO, and he would begin his battle procedure for the Battalion. If enemy numbers were low enough, Patrols might have a shot at the title, and deal with the threat themselves. But it all took time, and in the cold, no one was in the mood to sit around with no Bergens or sleeping bags. "What the Battalion is going to do," continued Tony, "is move in as close as 10km, and then rest up until Patrols make their report." He paused. "So get ready to push forward. Questions?" In the darkness, all he saw was shaking heads. He moved back up the line. Danny sat tight, waiting for us to move off, so he could count us, and then join on the end.

Reluctantly, we shed our warm kit, and got our shit sorted for another six kilometres, before we rested up again. It was now so cold; my leather gloves no longer insulated my hands, and were now just a cold layer around them. My feet were not faring much better, but hey, if you can't take a joke, Archie boy, you shouldn't have joined. After a short while, all you could hear around us was cursing and groaning, and some were not being all that quiet about it. Everyone started to get to their feet. Danny approached the individuals causing the commotion. I couldn't hear what he said to them, but they were rather reserved after his little visit.

We started the march again, slowly shuffling forward, and I was expecting the guys leading the way to open the pace again, but it never came. The whole pace and mood had now shifted to the task at hand, the capture of Teal Inlet. If the enemy soldiers were worth their pay, and were as daring as their pilots, they could have troops out almost as far as we were roaming, security for their commanders in Teal, who knows? Any enemy spotters would be in for a nasty shock, to come around the corner and see over 600 cold, wet British troops just wanting a brew and a fag, heavily armed coming towards them. The Battalion had its business head on now, slow and methodical, we didn't want to run up the backside of Patrols, and at worst have another friendly fire incident, because everyone was on the lookout for Argies.

The pace, easy as it was now, still caused me to sweat like a maniac, since with the exception of drinking some of my water, and scoffing some of my food, my gear remained the same weight as when we left San Carlos. My feet were really starting to give me some discomfort now, and starting to feel rather raw. I started to think about the possible battle ahead, would I perform? Would we all survive? Would we get ambushed in the next gully? One thing after another. We made our way off some high ground and into what looked like a rather wide and shallow valley of sorts. As we got lower, I could see guys having trouble with their footing, and before long, we were trudging through bog and surface water again. Everyone was almost at a standstill, and word came down the line that we had a river crossing. Great, as if we weren't piss-wet through already. When it came to my turn, just as I got ready to skip across, Jamie piped up, "If you fall over, that will be so funny."

"Shut up, you dick," I retaliated. I managed to get across, soaked from the knees down. Not great, but better than being sat in it, since it was now so fucking freezing. Jamie, the tosser, fared about the same. We continued to move forward, and as we started to climb out of the valley, we encountered a series of wire cattle fences. We followed one for a short while, until everyone stopped. The moon was out, and I could see quite clearly that large groups of troops were being led over to other parts of the valley, probably the other companies. But we stayed put. This time, with no waiting around, I dived straight into my barrel bag for the prized quilted jacket, and it was on in a flash, magic! I fished out some chocolate from my smock, and shared it with Jamie. I looked left and right of me; the lads were getting as comfy as possible, pulling out their ponchos and attaching them to the fence, making a very crude bivouac site.

John came down the line and called our Section in. "Get yourselves sorted out, Patrols are on task now. We are going to be here for a while. We are just 9km shy of Teal. Get as much rest as you can. No white light. Smoke if you want, but don't take the piss. And no cooking, understand?"

We nodded, just keen to rest and sort our feet out. Jamie and I used both our ponchos. I attached mine to the fence, and his was used as a groundsheet. Taking all that kit off was like a gift from the gods. As I took my webbing off, I felt like I was going to float away, and it felt so good to be more nimble again, without all that gear on. I wasted no time getting my quilted trousers on, as well as my waterproofs, just as another layer between me and the cold night air. We arranged our bivouac with our weapons in the middle, and our webbing acting as a pillow. Having my quilted suit on felt great, and my waterproofs made them windproof. Before I could attempt to get some sleep, I had to change my socks, one foot at a time, should the bad guys come looking for us. I peeled my right boot off, and I slowly peeled off my sock, so I didn't disturb what blisters I may have produced. Having such cold feet for most of the march, they had grown numb, which in turn could mask any potential blister problems. In the dark, I carefully rubbed my hand over my bare foot, to find rather surprisingly only a couple of small blisters; one on the heel, and one on my big toe. On the march, they felt bloody massive, but now I felt like a bit of a fraud. I wrung my sock out as much as I could and stuffed it under my right armpit, the aim of which was for my body heat, what there was of it, to eventually dry the sock. For a few minutes, I massaged my foot back to life, before fetching dry socks I had stowed inside my barrel bag. With a dry sock now on, I replaced my boot, since I had no trainers with me, and leaving my boots off would be a bad move, because firstly, I couldn't react to an enemy attack very effectively, and secondly, my feet would swell, and getting my boots back on would be torture. Besides, having John catch me without my boots on was a real motivator for wearing them. I repeated the routine with my left foot, job done, time to settle down and try to get some kip. But the half-frozen ground made sleep pretty much impossible. The cold seeped through my clothing, and after a while I began to shiver, my feet like blocks of ice once again. Jamie fared no better. He was of a slighter frame than me, and so I reckoned he felt the cold more. I ended up in the foetal position, facing inwards with my arms folded, trying to preserve as much warmth as I could. Jamie rolled over and adopted the same position, but facing me. He looked at me, and I could make out a grin amongst his cam creamed face. "Fancy a cuddle?"

"You are such a knob," I replied. He sat up and rubbed his hands together, then started rooting through his kit for food. "This was not in the brochure," he stated. "I didn't see this on the bloody recruiting poster."

We had no idea how long we would be there, but I had to admit, the Patrols guys were something else. They had walked the same route we had, and there was the CTR to do as well. Good bunch of operators. The more switched

72

on members of the Battalion went to Patrols, since it would be them talking directly to the CO via radio, describing to him what they could see on the target. Integrity and honesty was the name of the game with them guys, since the CO would act according to the information they gave him. I doubt the CO was getting much kip either, planning the potential battle ahead.

I started to drift in and out of sleep. The wind had dropped but the cold remained. I opened one eye, and over Jamie's shoulder, I could see frost settling on Brandon and Kyle's poncho. My breath was even more prominent in the cold air. I could tell Jamie was still alive, because I could see his breath emerging from his nostrils. Some of the other guys had given up trying to sleep, and had done away with the cigarette, cooking and white light discipline. All around our position, I could see light glowing under ponchos, where they had the kettle on. To heat up hot water and our rations, we were issued a hexamine cooker each. It was a very crude but effective piece of kit, a small flimsy metal frame that you unfolded to make a cooking hob. Inside was a pack of basically what can be described as a box of firelighters, like what you would have for your barbecue, hexamine tablets. You'd light one and put your mess tin full of water on to heat up. Some instead used the metal mug that fitted over the top of your water bottle. Hey presto, water would hopefully be at the boil in a matter of minutes. Seeing everyone around me getting hot food and brews on the go, I sat up and thought *fuck it*. I got my brew kit and some porridge out of my webbing, and got it all on the go. I gave Jamie a shove. He took one look at what I was up to, and quickly looked around for any sign of swift reprisal. He grinned and chuckled. "Great idea, Batman, John is going to do his nut."

"Don't think so, there's a burner going under his poncho too."

"Gleaming." I think everyone got to a point where slowly freezing to death was not an option. Besides, we were out of sight of Teal, and God forbid the Argie patrol that might crash this tea party. Jamie reached into his webbing and fished out his porridge, and placed it next to mine, since I'd already assumed the title of chef. He then grabbed my brew kit, and poured a sachet of hot chocolate into the mug. Soon we had porridge on the go, with a drop of chocolate in it, and to finish off, two big sachets of sugar, gorgeous. We took our time eating our porridge, and the brew went back and forth many times between us, we didn't want it to end.

Once finished, and our gear packed away, we'd had enough of lying on a freezing cold floor, and emerged from our poncho to get the blood circulating again. I just jogged on the spot for a few minutes, whilst Jamie did a series of jumps, knees to chest, just to warm up. It must have been contagious. After a while, everyone got out of their ponchos and did the same. Some got cigarettes on the go and visited other ponchos, shooting the shit, though everyone took their weapons wherever they went, still preserving some professionalism. We didn't venture too far. No real reason, it was just too cold to be sociable. "My round," Jamie announced. He went back under the poncho to get his brew kit fired up, magic.

Then I noticed Brandon walking up the line, poking his head into each poncho as he went, clearly talking to the occupants. He pulled up at ours with some news. "Second Battalion TABbed south tonight, and are in a serious scrap as we speak, about twenty k's south of San Carlos."

Jamie's head was already outside the poncho. "Seriously?"

Brandon nodded. "John told me to spread the word."

"Casualties?" I asked.

"Some," he murmured. "No names yet, I'm sure we will find out soon enough." He continued on his rounds, and I ducked under the poncho for the hot chocolate. In silence,

75

we sipped it in turns. We all knew guys in the first and second battalions. Our training platoon was split amongst the battalions, when we passed out of training. Casualties, now that made things very real. This wasn't just going to be strong talk in Westminster, and we knew the Navy had taken a battering already, but for troops to be in action on the ground this soon, Maggie wasn't fucking around.

John poked his head in our poncho, scaring the shit out of us. "Pack your shit; we are moving now, no one's home." We looked at him blankly, not too sure how to take the news. "Patrols have reported back. Any Argies that had been there fucked off days ago, and there appears to be none in the area as far as they are concerned, now get ready to move." He walked off down the line, and we quickly downed the remains of our brew, and started packing our gear in quick time. The frost had really settled on my poncho, to a point that I had to really work the material, so I could pack it away in my barrel bag. All over the valley, you could see troops getting packed, ready for the move into Teal. Light began to appear in the east, as the sun started to come up, and you could see everyone's breath in the cold morning air.

I went through the rigmarole of getting my kit back on my cold stiff frame, for the last push into Teal. Once geared up, we both sat leaning against the fence line, waiting for the order to move out. In the meantime, I thought about our Second Battalion. They must have set off about the same time we did, but clearly on a different route. Was it a deliberate action? Or did they encounter the enemy on their axis of advance. Nothing they couldn't handle, I'm sure, but for their battle to still be in full swing was a sobering thought, considering that in less than a couple of hours, it would be broad daylight. I had professional envy for them, since they had the first bite at the cherry as it were, but to know that they had casualties, and were continuing to take them, was something I wasn't in so much of a rush to envy.

Everyone started to get to their feet, groaning like old men getting out of their favourite chairs. I hooked my arms over the fence so I could get myself to my feet, but the wire had got caught on my barrel bag, and was now stuck. I was half-squatting against the fence. Jamie just watched and giggled. "Don't be a dick," I barked, and held my hand out for some assistance.

He grabbed my forearm, and reached behind me with his other hand to untangle me from the fence. Once I was free, he helped me upright, and then handed me the Gimpy and my helmet. "Here you go, mate," he said, winking.

"Nice one," I replied. "Let's get going, I'm bloody freezing." Our platoon started to move off, not entirely sure if we were still in the order of march. All around the valley, columns of troops were slowly making their way over to our side, as we climbed a gentle gradient. As it levelled out in the far distance, you could see Teal Inlet, the morning sun reflecting off the roofs of the small number of buildings that made up the settlement. If it wasn't for the biting cold, you could mistake it for the mirage of an oasis, sat amongst some distant sand dunes. Gimpy on my shoulder, we followed a series of fence lines. It was as good as daylight now, and since it was revealed there was no enemy in the area, the Battalion slogged it out, just to get into Teal as soon as possible. I was soon starting to leak sweat again, since the exertion of the march started to heat up my body, under all of my equipment. But it didn't matter; we had ahead of us the potential promise of shelter, hot water, and hopefully somewhere decent to get some kip.

CHAPTER 4: News from Goose Green

Teal Inlet wasn't much to write home about if I'm honest, but on this day it had to be one of the best things I had seen for the last couple of days. It was pretty much just a large farm complex, which consisted of the main building and several smaller houses, along with large sheep sheds, paddocks and pens. The march into Teal was pretty much uneventful. We had covered some gentle rolling moorland, with the odd stream to cross, but nothing outrageous. The lead companies were already in the settlement, snapping up the best spots to bivouac up, but we had already been given our area to set up shop. As much as the Battalion would love to cram into the buildings in order to get out of the cold, and grab a bed and a bath, this was clearly not going to happen. Besides the fact there wasn't enough room for us all, we were not too far away from enemy forces with a very active air force. Our column came to a halt, and it wasn't long before we were led over to our bivvy area. There was a small cluster of trees at Teal which I found rather bizarre, since we had covered a considerable distance of just bare-arsed terrain. These are prime bivvy spots, and the Patrols boys had the monopoly on this real estate. Can't say I blame them; they'd been working their arses off since leading us out of San Carlos.

79

As Jamie and I were sited by Danny, I took a look around. There were people stood around chatting, getting brews on the go, and smoking cigarettes. A few others were swinging picks and shovels about, getting their positions sorted. We took off all our gear and enjoyed the weightlessness for a couple of minutes, before having a stretch-off, working out aching shoulders and backs. The weather was starting to close in, and it wouldn't be long before the heavens would open, so Jamie and I broke out the digging tools before we got any cooking on the go. It wasn't long before we were just above shin-deep into the ground, and just over knee-deep with the spoil built up around three sides of our trench. We left the bottom end of it unspoiled, so getting in and out would be easier. The trench was deep enough to get out of the wind, and wide and long enough for us both to lay down when it was time to sleep. We then put Jamie's poncho down as a groundsheet, and used mine as the overhead cover. Being next to a fence line was a nice touch, since fitting my poncho above our trench was made all the more easier. Once complete, it was time to get cooking. Jamie broke out his hexi burner and brew kit, and I rummaged through my webbing for what was left of our rations.

"We should get more rations today," Jamie said as he stirred the brew, "and our Bergens with a bit of luck."

We sat under our poncho while we ate, and the fog was starting to drift into the settlement from the sea. With the fog came a light spattering of rain on our poncho, nothing heavy, but you could tell it was in for the rest of the day. I wasn't too fussed by this, I had waterproofs and quilted suit, which would do me OK until I got my Bergen back. A pair of boots appeared at the end of our trench, and Kyle peered under the poncho. "Alright boys? Grab your weapons; the OC wants to talk to the Company."

We clambered out of our position, and followed everyone else to the end of our Company line. It wasn't a defensive position as such, and the Company was crammed along a series of fence and gorse lines. Most of the Company had formed in a big huddle; no one was stood in three ranks, like what would have happened back in Tidworth. I looked around at the guys. We'd been on the islands literally a matter of days, and we all looked like we'd been on the Russian Front for a year. We were all filthy, from mud through digging in, and sleeping in trenches in just what we were wearing. Many of us had dry salt patches on our smocks from the effort of last night's march. All in high spirits, but we just looked like we were in shit state. I peered into the OC's position, since he had his poncho pitched higher than most, and I could see him chatting away into his radio handset to someone. In between exchanges, he was sipping on a brew. "Right, listen up fellas!" Dale shouted above the din of a Company shooting the shit. We all then became silent. "The OC wants to address you guys on events that have taken place since we left San Carlos," continued Dale. "After that, 6 Platoon, followed by 5, then 4 with all HQ elements will go over to the main farm building, where the lady of the house is dishing out hot chocolate and fried egg sarnies. Don't rip the arse out of it, but please go have some. The OC has been informed that our Bergens will be here by last light, so yes it will be another rummage in the dark for our gear, but we will be sleeping in our bags tonight, fingers crossed. Platoon sergeants, be ready with a work party to get the rations off the tractors when they arrive, and there will be jerry cans of water available as well. Whilst down at the house, get your water bottles filled there, since it will probably taste better than the sterilized stuff we have. Questions?"

No one had any; I think we just had our minds set on fried egg sandwiches. The OC was now stood next to Dale, who nodded to him and stood to one side. "Thanks Sergeant Major," Justin began. "Gentlemen, I would first like to thank you for your efforts in getting us here. I understand the pace at times was rather tasty, but I'm sure it's nothing you lot can't handle. Our guys that fell out of the march will be arriving with the tractors tonight, so let's make sure they have somewhere to sleep, and that they get back into Company routine as soon as possible. No doubt they will be a source of entertainment for some of you, but bear in mind we start walking again tomorrow, since the CO is keen to push east as soon as possible, and get eyes on the enemy." He paused. Jamie and I looked at each other with raised eyebrows. "The Second Battalion," continued Justin, "moved south from San Carlos, shortly after we moved east yesterday, and are now at the settlement known as Goose Green. It was heavily defended, and a long fight for it took place, which resulted in a large number of casualties. Among their dead are their Commanding Officer and their Adjutant." The fact that he mentioned the word 'dead' had us all open-mouthed, never mind the fact that their CO and Adj had been killed. "The Regimental Sergeant Major has the casualty list down at the main house," he stated. "When you go down there later, feel free to look at it. No doubt you will recognise some of the names, since the battalion have reported fifteen killed, and almost fifty wounded. The enemy however took one hell of a beating, but their dead and wounded have yet to be established, and over a thousand of them were taken prisoner." He paused again, acknowledging a mixture of bowed heads, and smiles and backslapping through regimental pride. "In summary, gentlemen, we have met

83

the enemy, and they have been found wanting. They are not a match for a professional, fit and aggressive army such as ours, but don't think that they will be a walkover. Give them a bloody nose. They are not so keen for it afterwards. If there are no questions, enjoy your sandwiches."

We all walked back to our positions, everyone a mixed bag of emotions; sorrow for the guys that had been killed and wounded, pride that the Regiment had once again shown they were the right guys for the job, but also professional jealousy that Second Battalion had got their hands dirty first. It was clear now that we had all, as a nation, gone well past talking our way out of this mess. We were now clearly at war, and I don't think we'd been in it this deep since Korea.

John came walking down the Section line. "Weapons and smocks only boys, and if you've got shaving kits, bring 'em too." My shaving kit was in my Bergen, not that I needed it in any particular hurry, but I was rather looking forward to brushing my teeth. You know when you have ripped the arse out of it, when you can taste your own breath. I picked up the Gimpy, and kept the belt of 100 on it, but wrapped the belt around the body of the gun, so it didn't swing all over the place. Gun on shoulder, we made our way towards the main building, where cooking was clearly on the go, smoke billowing constantly out of a chimney.

As we got close to the house, I noticed a group of guys stood outside the front door. They were smoking, and generally just chewing the fat. At first I thought they were the farmers from the settlement, but as I got closer, it was clear that farming was the furthest thing from their minds. They were heavily bearded, with various lengths of hair, a mixture of military and civilian ski-bobble hats on their heads. Their civilian duvet jackets wouldn't have looked out of place at Everest base camp. They wore combat trousers and civilian walking boots, and to top off their image, they had a mixed bag of American weapons, and the odd Gimpy for good measure. They looked pretty menacing to me, but that instantly faded when John shook their hands, wrapped his arm round one of them, and gave him a mock jab on the jaw. I looked over to Davo. He must have read the look on my face. "SF," Davo grinned, "probably ex-Third Battalion."

This was my first look at our Special Forces. Not quite what I had in mind, but they looked like they meant business. Despite looking like heavily-armed farmers, they clearly had a purpose here, and if I was a betting man, I'd bet they were here at Teal to dish out something nasty in the area. Whilst John was chatting to them, Charlie, our

Commanding Officer, came out of the front door, and gathered with the SF guys. After a brief chat and shaking of hands, the CO led them into the house, clearly for a more sensitive discussion, and John walked back over to us with a rare grin on his face. "Haven't seen Kev for years, didn't realise he'd done Selection." Selection was the notorious course to get into SF. Getting into the Parachute Regiment was tasty enough, but Selection was in a league of its own, not for the faint hearted.

We joined the back of a long queue, which was filing past what appeared to be the kitchen window, since I doubt the lady of the house wanted us lot filing through her gaff with muddy boots on. As I got to the window, a lad not much younger than me, probably the son, handed me a lukewarm egg sandwich and a mug of hot chocolate. The mug was fucking hot! I nearly dropped it, but I managed a quick regain. I thanked him, and behind him I could see what I could only guess were his sister and his mum, beavering away with cooking and hot chocolate making, trying to keep up with demand.

As we moved around the back of the house, there was chaos. Troops were everywhere, most stripped to the waist, around oil drums with big bowls of hot water on top, shaving soap plastered all over their faces. I didn't need to strip down, which I was pleased about, since a thick cold fog had well and truly arrived at the settlement. The sandwich was cold by the time I found a spot to put the gun down and tuck in. I wasn't going to complain, since it was either a cold egg sandwich, or dehydrated beef stew from our ration packs. The hot chocolate was bang on; I sipped it slowly, not wanting to finish it. I slowly took in the detail of the scene around me. Half-naked troops shaving in the freezing fog. The washing line that belonged to the family was overloaded with various items of military clothing. There were weapons and webbing all over the place. Some troops were smoking whilst cleaning weapons, some sorting their feet out, some nearer the house digging trenches. Teal was really a mixed bag of activity. Through the thick fog out in the bay, you could just make out shipping that had arrived, probably loaded with stores and all sorts of nasty stuff to fight the bad guys with. I hadn't even seen an Argentine soldier yet, but I'm sure it wouldn't be long, one way or the other.

"Platoon sergeants to me!" Dale yelled, over the din of troops milling about and shooting the shit. Everyone quietened down, probably intending to eavesdrop on Dale's talk with Danny and the other sergeants.

We were too far away to make out what they were saying, but judging by the sergeants scribbling furiously into their notebooks as Dale dictated, something was on the cards. They dispersed, and the sergeants including Danny called for their platoons to gather around them. In less than a minute, whatever their state of dress or stage of shaving, everyone was in their relevant huddle to receive information.

Danny waited patiently for us all to get in a spot, where we could see and hear him clearly. "Guys, Second Battalion's casualty list, only the dead at this time, but I'm sure word about the wounded will be around soon enough." He had everyone's undivided attention, as he read the names slowly and deliberately. Now and again, as he read out the full title of the soldiers killed at Goose Green, as in rank and full name, someone gave a low whistle or cursed under their breath. You could tell by some of the guy's reactions that they clearly knew these men, either through work, socially, or long-time friends. You could have knocked us over with a feather, because it wasn't until they read the names out, did the whole magnitude of what had taken place really sunk in. We were at war, we were killing each other, and it wasn't an exercise. I recognised one of the names, a Corporal that was my training NCO in Aldershot. To us, he was harsh but fair, proud of his regiment. He would do anything to preserve its reputation, and God forbid anyone that had another opinion about it, that wasn't to his liking. He was my instructor. I never really chatted to him, certainly never drank with him, apart from when my folks attended my passing-out parade at the end of training. In the NAAFI, which is basically a forces social club, he came over to where me and my parents were stood having a beer. He chinked my glass with his, informed my parents that I wasn't a bad kid, who should do OK in battalion, and walked off on his rounds, chatting to other parents. I had no real emotion over his death. In fact, I felt rather at peace, knowing that he had died in a matter that was probably to his liking, and wondered what happened to the Argentine soldier that had a hand in his death.

Danny snapped me out of it. "Lads, the Boss and OC are in with the CO, with regards to our possible move east tonight. Not sure when we will see our Bergens, but things are starting to heat up, and I'm not talking about the weather." He had a point. With the fog in, it was bloody freezing. "Get your shit together, and get ready for another long night. I will get more information to you as I find out more, crack on."

We dispersed, heading back to our ponchos. The main thing on my mind was getting a bit of rest before we started TABbing again. Just as we got back to our positions, I could hear engine noise getting louder, from the west side of the settlement. An annoying creaking and rattling of metal began. It was catching the attention of everyone around me, and it briefly crossed my mind that armoured vehicles were coming into town, whose was anyone's guess.

"Tractors are here," someone called out. The nervous suspense subsided instantly, as a long column of tractors and trailers arrived alongside the main settlement house. Some trailers were brimming with Bergens, with a few guys sat on top. Some tractors dragged pallets with missiles and all sorts of ammo, everything wrapped in cargo netting. One trailer was straining under the weight of tons of rations in brown cardboard boxes. Other tractors had trailers brimming with all sorts of randomness, but all I was interested in right now was the rations and my Bergen. Without being prompted, guys began to unload the Bergens, placing them into company lines for their owners to collect when allowed. The tractors dragging all the ammo were led down towards the water's edge, away from the buildings, which I assumed was because if Ayrton and his boys paid us a visit, we would not all go up in a colossal explosion of stacked ammunition. It was a good job the fog was in, to be fair. The ration trailer was being parked alongside a barn of sorts, and the guys formed a human chain, lugging to each other, emptying the trailer in quick time.

The hive of activity soon petered out, and I took the chance to grab my Bergen. It took a few minutes of scrabbling through what was left of our Company kit to find it. As I got back to my poncho, Jamie was sat outside it, squaring his feet away. Leighton and Kyle, along with Davo, were coming down the line, dropping off four boxes of 24hr rations and a couple of packets of hexamine fuel at each poncho, one less chore for us to do. Zane came over puffing and panting with two full jerry cans of water for our Section, which he placed down next to us. If anyone wanted to fill water bottles, they now didn't have to travel far, because our poncho was in the middle of our Section position.

John was nowhere to be seen. Someone had called for all section commanders, whilst the tractors were being unloaded. No doubt they were being briefed up on tonight's activities. Once I'd sorted my feet out, powdered, and had fresh socks and my beloved trainers on, I felt like a new man. I thought I'd better give the Gimpy a bit of care and attention. By rights, what should happen is weapon, kit, self, but I was already halfway through sorting my feet out, when I noticed some of the guys stripping and cleaning their weapons. The gun only needed a quick spruce, because I hadn't fired the thing since we got ashore. Apart from a little bit of rust here and there, which I quickly dealt with, using one of the wire brushes in my cleaning kit, she was good to go. A quick lick of oil on the working parts, and Robert was your mother's brother.

Jamie and I broke open the new rations, and squeezed them into our webbing. Some goodies went into smock pockets, for quick access during the TAB. We stowed all our gear, including our Bergens, under our poncho. We flat-packed the cardboard from the ration packs, lining the bottom of our position for a bit of insulation, from the cold earth under the poncho. After rearranging our kit a few times, like moving furniture around a small room, we got the kettle on for a well-earned cup of tea.

We'd just brewed up and got comfy, when Davo stuck his head under our poncho. "Boss is back, just come as you are."

We clambered out. Tony and John were stood a little away from the Section ponchos. We all gathered around them, the remainder of the platoon being rounded up by Danny. After a couple of feet-stamping minutes in the cold, Tony addressed us. "Guys, the Commanding Officer is keen for us to march east to a settlement called Estancia tonight, 26 K's away." There were a few sighs, but business was business. "SF has put any move east out of bounds until at least 0600 hours tomorrow, because they have some business to take care of first, which will make our move to Estancia free of enemy. So as it stands, we will be stopping here tonight, and now we have our Bergens, life will be a little more comfortable, at least for now. Patrols are to move off east at 0615, and once they have established a suitable lead, we will then move off. Bergens will stay here again, and the tractors will follow on with them later. Questions?"

There were none. As the boss walked off, me and Jamie high-fived, and got back under our poncho, wrestling with our Bergens, forcing them to give up their precious booty called sleeping bags.

Once all snug in my bag, I was rather relieved that we were not pushing forward that night, since sleep was on my list of priorities. Besides, SF had some business to take care of, and far be it for me to rush them. I drifted in and out of sleep as the evening wore on, due to the fact that there was still a lot of activity going on around the settlement; tractors moving about, people calling out, etc.

Sometime later, I felt my shoulder being given a shove. "Mate, here you go." I rolled over, and Jamie was handing me food and brew. I sat up, my head brushing the underside of the poncho. Once I managed to focus a bit better, I accepted breakfast in bed.

"What time is it?" I asked.

"Half six," he replied. "You slept straight through." I rested my head back on my webbing, and gave out an almighty stretch. A whole night's kip without any guard duty. How did that happen? Clearly, Jamie didn't get pinged for one either, because he would have put my name on the list for good measure, or would have dragged me out of bed to keep him company for a cold hour or so. I propped myself up a bit more, so I could eat and drink without wearing half of it. It was a very cold morning, our breath very prominent in the air under our poncho. Jamie was still in his bag, eating away at a leisurely pace, watching the world go by. Not that there was much of a world going by at this time. There were a few people moving about, tractors moving around behind us, and the odd helicopter zooming over, but nothing to get excited about.

As I took in more of the sweet tea Jamie had lovingly prepared, I noticed a pair of legs arrive at his side of the poncho. Davo knelt down, and with a grin he rested on his side, and helped himself to Jamie's cup of tea. "Listen up lads. The commandos will be arriving shortly, and we need to make room for them. Patrols left some time ago, and have now established themselves some distance away to the east, towards Estancia House. We will be leaving in a little while, so get your gear together. More details to follow, OK?"

He left. I didn't want to get out of my bag, since it was bloody freezing outside, but orders were orders, and we had business of our own to take care of. Once breakfast was finished, we forced ourselves out of our bags and into our quilted suits in record time. We already knew we wouldn't be taking Bergens again for this move, so our packing routine was pretty much the same as when we TABbed out of San Carlos. We packed everything away, including our ponchos, and sat on our Bergens in front of our hole, with our marching kit placed in front of us. Looking left and right, others had pretty much done the same. A light fog hung in the air, so you couldn't see the whole settlement. Out in the bay, I could just make out the outline of a ship or two. I just hoped the Argy air force wasn't knocking about and hadn't noticed them, or else this morning was going to be a repeat of San Carlos the other day.

People started shouting up the line. Bergens were to be taken over to Dale's position, and with smocks and weapons only, we did just that. We hung around by the Bergen stack, shooting the shit with a few of the guys we hadn't seen for a couple of days. One of them pointed out a rather bizarre sight on the outskirts of the settlement. In the light fog appeared what I thought was livestock, wandering in between the buildings. Very quickly it was clear that these huge lumbering beasts were in fact human beings. As they drew closer, you could make out weapons in their hands and green berets on. The commandos had arrived. They looked completely shattered. The lead one stopped moving and leant back, slumping to the floor. A few of our lads ran over to help him. The Marines lined up behind him did the same. Our guys helped them loosen their Bergen straps. They must have walked the whole route so far with Bergens.

More staggered into Teal, very tired. It was clear this was maybe the commandos we encountered on the way out of San Carlos, who had moved north. They got themselves sorted out into company lines and removed their Bergens. They went straight into admin, sorting their feet out. A few just sat on the ground, enjoying a cigarette. "Right, shows over, let them get themselves sorted," Dale shouted. "Get back to your positions and get ready to move."

As we walked back to our positions, I don't think I heard anyone take the piss out of the commandos. Such an opportunity is rarely allowed to go to waste, but seeing them stagger into the settlement with all that kit on maybe humbled a few of us. The commandos were tough, make no mistake. I think we just appreciated the fact that our

Commanding Officer wanted his paratroopers to move quick and light, even if it meant being colder as a result.

"Kit on," Danny shouted out, "follow me." With all my kit on once again, I shuffled it about, so it would sit comfortably for the march ahead. With my helmet on and Gimpy on my shoulder, I followed Jamie and the rest of the platoon to the eastern side of the settlement, where the Company was gathering. Leaning on a fence, we could see the commandos taking up residence in our previous trenches, one less thing for them to do before they got in their sleeping bags, I supposed.

Slowly but surely, the Battalion began its march east once again, en route to a settlement called Estancia House, 26 kilometres away.

CHAPTER 5: The Cool Clean Throne

It wasn't long before a cracking pace was set again. I was sweating like a maniac, gun on shoulder, trying to keep up. The terrain hadn't changed; long uphill gradients, low boggy grass, numerous river crossings, and ankle-deep tussock grass, which really gave your feet some stick. Every hour we stopped for a few minutes, before setting off again.

At one particular rest stop, I noticed mountain ranges were starting to appear. On HMS Intrepid, we had a series of briefs about the layout of the islands. Their capital, Port Stanley, was surrounded by mountains, so I guess we weren't that far from there. I'm not sure if it was due to my sweat cooling when we rested, but it really was starting to get colder.

We set off again, two columns of troops stretching out ahead of me, everyone fighting their own loads, the radio operators with their Bergens struggling to keep up with their rather energetic commanders. I was content with my lot in life right now, just a gunner lumbering along, with Jamie as my ammo donkey.

It was starting to get dark when we stopped again. Danny and John came up the line, letting us know that Patrols were now checking out Estancia. Early reports showed that there was no enemy there. Result, I wasn't in the mood for a scrap right now. Same routine as before, we got as comfy as possible, waiting for Patrols to give us the nod to move into the settlement. Quilted suit and fresh socks on, Jamie and I got a hot chocolate on the go, and just talked about random shit as it presented itself. Some of the lads found a fence line to set up their ponchos and try and get some kip, but it was far too cold for that. We chose to just sit there and keep warm with brews.

Danny and the Boss came up the line, and called the platoon together. Jamie was dispatched by Danny to turf some guys out from their ponchos, which was not the most popular task in the world. But they would ignore Jamie at their peril, because the following wake-up call would be by Danny, who had his own method of swift justice.

We all gathered. "Guys," Tony began "we are now very much on the enemy's doorstep. Estancia is clear for us, so we will be moving shortly. Same drill as before when we get there, but as before, don't expect a long stay. There will be no more lounging around, as we did in Teal. We will almost be on the FLET, and with this is the possibility of counterattack. Any questions?"

There were none. FLET meant Forward Line of Enemy Troops, basically the front of the enemy positions, which meant at anytime from here on in, there was a real chance of encountering the enemy, carrying out their patrols.

The cold was really getting to us, as we waited for the Company to head off on the last stretch into the settlement. The column started to shuffle forward, and believe it or not, it was rather nice to get back into our usual TABbing stride, since this kept the cold at bay until our next rest stop.

Off to our right side as we moved into the settlement was the beginning of a large series of hills, and I hoped the enemy wasn't watching our every move, as we slogged along with all our kit on. I remembered the Boss saying something about SF making sure our move would be enemy-free, when they had finished a particular task they were undertaking. I just hoped they got it done before we showed up.

We got into Estancia in the early hours, and were very quickly guided into our areas by the lads from Patrols. Battalion Headquarters had set up shop in the main building, lucky for them. As usual, us company peasants got given a fence line to pitch our ponchos on. We got put into position by Danny, who said for us to rest up, no briefs to be had as of yet, so maximum rest, no fucking about. Jamie and I went about our usual routine, shelter sorted, quilted suits on, then quick inspection of our feet. Mine were not looking too clever, the constant wet and increasing cold from the last march again had my feet looking like I'd spent too long in the bath. I made sure I gave them a good foot rub before I put dry socks on. I only had clean ones in my Bergen, but dirty ones were dry, all the same. Once done, I settled down on Jamie's freezing cold poncho. I was tired, but sleep was impossible, it was just too damn cold. At this point, I was noticing that my lower back and hips were very sore, partly due to weight loss perhaps, but also from my webbing belt. Not much I could do about it right now. Besides, I'm sure there were a lot of the guys nursing similar injuries, if not worse. A few guys were hiding injuries, such as turned ankles from the initial march out of San Carlos. The pride of some people!

I drifted in and out of sleep, but whenever I woke, I would shiver like mad, and try and tuck in closer to Jamie, not that he was any better off. In fact, he was probably colder than me, since I had more meat on the bone, and he was built like a jockey's whip. "I'm not easy, you know," he mumbled through his hood.

"What?"

"You haven't even bought me a drink, and you're trying your luck." Comedy is all about timing, so I'm told, and Jamie always had time for it. I wanted a brew, but couldn't face having cold air whipping around under my armpits, where I had managed to retain some heat. I caught the aroma of tobacco and burnt matches; someone had clearly given up on the "sleep in a freezer" competition, and got a fag on the go. I rolled over onto a cold patch of ground, and saw numerous people laying under their ponchos with fags on the go, or stood up outside, smoking their heads off and stamping their feet. Being a non smoker, I didn't understand the morale aspect of having cigarettes in such circumstances. I'd smoked in training, but only because I thought it looked hard. When I got to battalion, it just faded away, like many of the hobbies I'd undertaken in my youth. I could hear more and more people moving about; the clatter of mess tins, a random heavy cough from under a poncho, numerous farts, and the usual dawn chorus of soldiers, trying to come to life in a frozen farmer's field. I rolled over to face Jamie, but all I was welcomed with was his left hand inside his hood, at which point it produced the hugest bogey I'd ever seen.

"You are such a charmer," I giggled.

"It's got to be your turn to do breakfast," he stated. I forced myself to sit up and shift around, to get at my webbing. I dug out the gear required for a feast, and got the water on the go. Jamie sat up, hood still up, and he then scrambled out of his side of the poncho, probably for a morning piss.

With water coming to the boil, I sorted us a big sweet cup of coffee and bacon grill. The sun had started to rise at this stage, and I became more aware of what was around us. Clambering out of the poncho for a big stretch, I looked around. The settlement appeared a lot smaller than Teal. It was just overwhelmed by ponchos, pitched up all over the place. For a professional army, we looked more like a refugee camp. Someone had already found time to exploit the main building washing line, with a random collection of socks and underwear hanging from it, and judging by the condition of those items, they definitely belonged to soldiers. Some guys braved the elements and were stripped to the waist shaving. I rubbed my hand over my own face, and it was clearly evident I would need to carry out the same ablution, once my Bergen caught up with us. I noticed a huge pile of cubed peat, stacked up outside of the main building, some of the lads taking the odd cube, and putting it into the few stoves available in the courtyard.

I noticed Danny walking up the platoon line, telling the boys to get up, and get squared away. As he got to our poncho, he seemed happy that at least some of his soldiers were up and moving. "Don't wander too far; the Boss is in with the OC, with regards to our next move."

He walked on. Next move? Did this mean we had another TAB coming up? Or just what was going to be happening around here? I wasn't feeling the love for another TAB just yet. I just wanted my Bergen, a shave, fresh socks, and a nice, long warm kip, and in that order too. There wasn't much to do now, other than wait for the Boss's orders and our Bergens. At this time my stomach turned over, which announced that it was time for me to do something about it. I quickly rummaged through my kit, and found some toilet paper. I grabbed the Gimpy and made off to the main building for my call of nature. It was a long shot, but the worst they could say was no. I made my way to the door at the rear of the building, since I'm sure the lady of the house wouldn't appreciate Archie from Portsmouth bounding in through the main door, asking for the shitter. I knocked on the door which led directly to the kitchen, but no one responded, so I took a chance and slowly opened the door. As I peered through the gap, I could see a lot of people, including our OC and the heavily armed farmers from Hereford, poring over a map on the kitchen table.

"Can we help you, mate?" said a voice to my right. It gave me such a fright, my package almost made a premature appearance.

I looked round, and one of the SF guys was leaning against the door frame, with a radio handset to his ear. I made my pathetic plight to him. "Erm, toilet?"

"Front door mate, now piss off!"

Door shut, I made my way around to the front door, calling myself a dickhead for representing myself and my Regiment in such a poor light, like a scruffy orphan asking for the scraps from the masters' table. I approached the front door with less caution, and even though I knocked, I made my way in. The house was a hive of activity. Officers pored over maps, signallers listening intently to radio traffic, the lady of the house doing the rounds with a tray of hot drinks. I managed to make eye contact with her, and she looked me up and down, smiling as she shook her head, indicating the toilet with a head jerk and a raised eyebrow. I locked myself in and stripped off all my warm kit, and parked my arse on the cool clean throne. Priceless!

I made sure I cleaned up after myself, not wanting this gift from the gods to be removed from us, due to the odd soldier not respecting the facility. As I made my way to the front door, the lady, whom I never got to speak to or even thank properly, gave me a thumbs up as I left. Thank you! As I got back to my poncho, no one was around, and then it suddenly dawned on me that I'd disobeyed Danny. Fear and dread filled me instantly, you don't ignore him.

"Archie!" I spun on my heels and saw Jamie waving me over, to where the whole Platoon was gathered around the Boss's poncho. I dashed over and plonked my arse down next to Jamie, not wanting to make eye contact with anyone. No such luck. As I glanced up, Danny was glaring straight at me. In an attempt to break his gaze, I looked over to John, who was glaring at me, just as intense. Not good. John had clearly received a bollocking from Danny, and this was not going to end well for me. I looked for comfort in the eyes of my Platoon commander, but he didn't appear in the mood for entertaining me either.

"Now that we are all together," Tony barked, "I will cover the details again, for young Archie's benefit." Mutterings of 'prick' and 'crow' were heard amongst the audience, as I looked at the ground for inspiration. At our feet was the Boss's map, and he had a pencil in his hand to point out various points during his delivery. "To orientate you to the map, this is where we are now, Estancia, and if you look over your right shoulder, you will see the summit of Mount Kent, which is here." Sorted, I was happy with where we are, willing him to get on with it. "SF and commandos, with the only remaining Chinook, took a daring bound forward the other night, and seized this vital summit from the enemy. After a brief but heavy contact, the enemy withdrew, and we now control the high ground overlooking our current position, hence the reason our move here was delayed. The last thing we need is to have our position under observation, and the threat of air and artillery attack." He paused to let it sink in. "Further to that, SF also destroyed a small garrison of enemy troops, at a place called Top Malo House, which if left untended, could have given us trouble from the right as we moved here, and could have also been used to mount raids against us, while we caught our breath." He pointed to the high ground, on the map and in situ. "These features now hide us from view, from the enemy defences around Port Stanley; Mount Estancia here, and Mount Vernet here. Once over the skyline of these features, we will be in full view of the enemy, and also their artillery footprint. Patrols Company will be pushing into no man's land tonight, to establish a patrol base at a place called Murrell Bridge. From there, we will receive CTR tasks for our next objectives. Any questions?"

"Fighting patrols?" asked John.

"Most likely," Tony replied, "we have to ensure our patrol programme doesn't clash with what the commandos have in mind, and the CO is keen for us not to have a repeat of what happened at San Carlos. Once Patrols have established our battle space and objectives, we will then build our patrol programme. Any other questions?" There were none. "Right then, guys. It's the real deal. We've got business to take care of. The CO wanted the Battalion to advance to contact, all the way into Stanley, but Brigade said no, as they want a Brigade action to take place shortly. They're just waiting for all the right pieces to get into place before we kick off. Get yourselves tidied up. Our Bergens should be here shortly."

Everyone started to disperse, but Danny pointed at me, and summoned me over. Sheepishly, I approached him. John came over as well. "Do I speak another language to you, do I?" demanded Danny.

"No Sergeant," I replied, awaiting my fate.

"Drop the Sergeant shit," he blasted, "you know that's not how I roll. Don't mug me off, you little fuck, or else the Argentines will be the least of your problems, do you understand me?"

"Yes, Danny."

"Right then," he berated. "When the tractors arrive, I hope you're feeling strong, because you are on Bergen detail, and my shit list for the rest of the day, so any poxy jobs need doing, you are on the top of my list, understand?" I nodded. "Besides, how the hell did you blag using the bogs in the house?" he demanded to know. "I went to use them," he moaned, "and some twat of an officer told me to go away."

I grinned. "My boyish charms."

"Well, they haven't helped you in this case, have they?" he observed. "Now piss off."

I legged it back to my position, before I pushed my luck too far. Jamie was getting the kettle on as I arrived. I mulled a few things over, as we waited for the water to boil. Things were getting serious, since the Boss was talking about things like battle space and fighting patrols.

From what I could gather, battle space was an area of ground in which the Battalion could operate, in theory without interference from other units. Hopefully, this would prevent friendly fire incidents. We tended to do most of our business in the dark, so clarity was important.

As for fighting patrols, I was more familiar with those. You went out in no less than platoon strength, so you were looking at least thirty plus troops. You would deliberately pick a fight with the enemy, giving them a bloody nose, lowering their morale, so their patrols, if they still took place, would not be effective, and therefore you would dominate no man's land. That term in itself seemed rather surreal. I couldn't help but think about the Somme, and the stretch of land between the trenches. The same principle applied, but with more land between them and us.

Jamie snapped me out of my thoughts. "What did he say?"

"I'm on his shit list, at least for the day."

"Don't be getting me roped into your unfortunate business," he stated, "I'm getting my Bergen, and getting my fat head right down."

"Don't be like that. Besides, many hands make light work, and all that."

"Piss off, drink your brew." It seemed that everyone was telling me to jog on today.

It wasn't long before the tractors came rattling and squeaking into town, so without waiting to be reminded, I got my weapon slung, and in just my smock began to make my way over to the main building. "Archie," hollered John, "take that skinny gob shite with you; you will only get lonely otherwise."

With great delight, I jogged back to our poncho to turf Jamie out. "You are such a wanker," he mumbled under his breath. He indicated John. "And him."

"Come on," I encouraged Jamie, "we get first dibs on our own kit, while we are there".

Same as Teal, the ammo tractors were led well away from where we were all kipping, and the buildings. Bergens were sorted in next to no time, and as we found our Platoon's kit, we put it to one side. Brandon and Zane took our kit back to our poncho for us. Then the rations got dumped on a sheep shed, along with any other weird and wonderful stuff that had made its way onto the trailers. We got a sweat on, but knowing we were merely minutes away from fresh socks and dry warm sleeping bags made it a worthwhile effort.

Returning to our position, admin was very much the order of the day. Everyone appeared to be enjoying having their Bergens back in their grubby mitts. I wasted no time getting my act together, since I was sure Danny had more shit jobs for me to do during the course of the day, so I needed to be quick and get some down time in the green maggot. Feet were done and dusted, with fresh socks and trainers on in record time. Straight away, ask any soldier, with fresh socks on in any part of the world, you do feel like

111

a new man. Then came the shave. There were some different schools of thought over this ablution. Some were hardcore and went for the cold water option. I was a big fan of this if the weather was favourable, but at Estancia House, with a freezing fog creeping in from the sea, I'm went the extra mile and boiled some water. Whilst the water was on the go, I dug deep into my Bergen, and fished out my shaving kit. Into the mess tin of water went my razor and shaving brush. Once the water was hot enough, in went the flannel, and I was on my way. A hot water shave is a lovely experience when you are in a cold place, Estancia more than qualified. Once the shave was over, I peered about and couldn't see anyone rushing to get cam cream on, so I thought I'd leave that to a more relevant time. Next on my to-do list was the Gimpy, not that she really needed it, so I gave her a quick wipe down and oiling, but I did take my time on the belts of ammo that had been draped over me for some time. I gave them a thorough wipe down, and carefully inspected them for rust. Once done, I filled my water bottles from my webbing, as the jerry can was once again in the middle of the Section line, next to our poncho. There were no more rations to dish out just yet, since wed been restocked at Teal.

Just as I was getting myself ready for bed, another bombshell hit our ears. "Dig in," Danny shouted up the line.

"Bollocks," I cursed under my breath, trying not to get overwhelmed with anger. I should have seen it coming. From a tactical point of view, digging in should have been the first thing we addressed, but I suppose these things happen in war. Fuck it, get on with it. Jamie was grinning at me, as he pulled back my poncho and peeled his off the floor. "What are you grinning at, you dick?" I growled.

"Your face is a picture," he chuckled. "I could see you all set for bed, and then wham!" I was raging, nothing worse than a sudden change of plan. I'm not the best soldier on the planet, but I do like routine, and if there is a sudden change when you're in your groove, it feels like the worst thing in the world. Heaven knows why I joined the Army. The term 'military precision' was thought up by someone who has never done a day in the military, and the term 'remain flexible' is just an officers' phrase, meaning they haven't got a clue what the fuck is going on. It was a good job I was paired up with Jamie, because he took the sting out of any shit situation, and as I calmed down, I did start to see the funny side of things.

It wasn't long before our earthworks were complete, and we set about getting all comfy again. Now in my sleeping bag, the last couple of hours didn't seem all that bad. Jamie got a brew on the go whilst sat up in his bag, and gave me the best hot chocolate I've ever tasted. I loved that guy, but I would never tell him. His head wouldn't fit under our poncho.

CHAPTER 6: The Plan to Take Mount Longdon

I woke with a start, fearing I'd missed another briefing by the Boss or Danny. As I looked left and right in the fading light, I could just see guys asleep under their ponchos, or stood about smoking and chatting. I leaned over, and could see Jamie was out for the count, so I just rested my head back on my webbing, and looked at the underside of the poncho above our heads. My breath in the cold foggy air was very prominent again, and the poncho had started to frost up. Why the guys were stood around chatting and stamping their feet was beyond me, since I'd have taken refuge in a sleeping bag hours ago. I looked at my watch; I'd certainly pushed out a few hours, with not so much of a shove from Danny with regards to my cock up earlier on. Danny was an OK guy, he wasn't one of them seniors that screamed and shouted, trying to shove everything. Airborne down your throat, don't get me wrong, he was proud of his Regiment, but he was a good operator, and did the job the way it should be done; either full on, or not at all. When Danny tore a strip off you, it wasn't a frenzied spit-flying rage, since troops get immune to that, and after a while it becomes a source of entertainment. The way Danny made you feel like a turd was by acting the disappointed father. And that cut me to the core, better than any screaming fit.

I just lay there planning world domination in my head, when I noticed John making his way up the line, stopping at every poncho on the way up, and peering underneath. I could hear muffled chat, but couldn't make out what was being said. I felt at ease that it wasn't a shit job from Danny on its way to me, since John knew exactly where I was sleeping, and would have come straight to me. Once he finished chatting with Kyle and Zane, he then moved over to us. As he arrived, I propped myself up on my right elbow, to receive whatever was coming. As he knelt down, he pulled back Jamie's hood on his sleeping bag. Jamie jumped out of his skin. "Relax, you idiot," John said, grinning. Something was up, if John was gentle and smiling. "Guys," he continued, "just to keep you in the picture, Patrols have now moved out towards Murrell Bridge, to establish a patrol base in that area. Our objective has been selected for us, it's a feature called Longdon." He paused, allowing it to slowly seep into our heads. "Patrols will begin to CTR Longdon, once they have established themselves at Murrell. More info to follow, any questions?"

As usual, there were none. Without ceremony, he stood up, and moved onto the next position. I lay back down with not much to think about, except the fact that we were looking at attacking this Longdon place pretty soon. I hadn't written home since we got there, mainly to do with being pretty busy in the last few days, and so far, with the exception of the air attacks at San Carlos, everything we'd done was not any different than any exercise I'd been on; TABbing, sweating, shivering, sleeping, eating, the usual stuff. I leant over to Jamie. "Do you think we will be attacking Longdon soon?"

"Mate, Patrols will take their time checking that place out before we go anywhere; we are going to be here for a while." He had a point. If the recce of Teal was anything to go by, the Patrols guys do like to take their time, and the last thing I wanted to do right now was rush them. They would go out of their way to ensure every enemy position was noted, since the last thing we needed was to encounter positions unmarked, since that could spell disaster in any attack. Take your time guys, take your time. The remainder of the night went without incident, but at one point, I'm sure I heard machinegun fire out in no man's land.

I came to at first light, and Jamie was sat up, getting his quilted suit on. "Get up mate, the Boss wants to talk to us." I lay back on my webbing, wishing the Boss would do a door-to-door information service, like John did last night.

I got myself out of my bag and into my quilted gear, since it was very cold that morning. I noticed Danny was calling for us to come as we were. Without waiting for him to get impatient, we jogged over to the Boss's poncho. We all gathered round, not wanting to sit on the frozen ground. Tony chose to stand when addressing us. "Guys, Patrols made contact with the enemy last night, in the area of Murrell Bridge. After a brief but fierce fire-fight, they managed to beat the enemy back, who withdrew in the direction of Mount Longdon. Patrols followed up with the intention of grabbing any enemy that was wounded in the exchange, but the enemy didn't hang around." Blimey, I thought, shit was really happening now. "No casualties suffered by our guys, thankfully," confirmed Tony. "Patrols are staying at Murrell, in order for us to dominate no man's land, and conduct operations from there. Pretty soon, they will have established our battle space, and then we can also patrol out there, and get a feel for the ground ahead.

"Behind the main building is an area taped off. No one is to go in there, since some of the Patrols guys will be coming back with information to build a model for the up-and-coming operations. More info will follow as we receive it. The CO also wants the companies to push out onto mounts Vernet and Estancia, so we can get eyes on the objective, Mount Longdon. Any questions?"

"When do we move up the hill?" John asked.

"No time has been given yet," answered Tony, "as said before, more info to follow." John nodded with satisfaction. "Right guys," the Boss continued, "it's very much a waiting game for the time being. Just keep yourselves busy and your gear squared away. Things could change very rapidly, and we may need to act fast. Speak to you later."

We made our way back to our positions, feeling at a bit of a loose end. Our admin was all done. We literally had not much to do. We couldn't check-fire our weapons, since that would blatantly advertise our location, so it was very much a case of twiddling our thumbs for the time being.

Over the next few days, things began to develop with regards to our mission. Guys from Patrols would move back to Estancia for rest, and also to begin construction of the earth model which would be used to deliver orders for the operation. Earth models are usually referred to as the Private soldiers' map, since it's normally just the commanders, ranging from Lance Corporal and above that possess maps and compasses, and if us Privates can see what the mission will entail, then we have a better understanding of what is required of us. The Patrols lads didn't spoil the area marked off for them with any digging, they brought in spoil from somewhere else in the settlement, and began to sculpt whatever it was they were trying to build. In its early stages, it was nothing more than just random piles of spoil all over the shop, and then a few days later, those piles were actually shaped to represent what was actually out in no man's land. They had one big pile of spoil, off the right of the smaller piles, and it then dawned on me what was taking place. The smaller piles were the area in general, and the big pile of spoil was Longdon in detail. Slowly but surely, more meat was being added to the bone.

Other members of the Battalion began patrolling out to our front, in order to build a better picture of what was out there. There was some Company activity out there, but I was not part of them patrols, the aim of which were to recce sites for fire-support teams, who would use machineguns and MILAN anti-tank systems. MILAN was a system that fired missiles on a wire, and the firer could control the missile by keeping the crosshairs on the target. A pulse signal was sent down the wire, which commanded the missile to move up and down, left and right. The enemy didn't have any armoured vehicles as far as we knew, so it was decided the missiles would be used to smash any bunkers or strong points we encountered. Snipers also moved out to our front with Patrols, and would loiter out there, reporting on what they observed, and kill key enemy personnel if the opportunity arose. Key personnel would include commanders, anyone that could be seen to be in charge. To the trained eye, your body language could give away the fact that you were a leader. Radio operators were also targets, the antenna sticking out of their backpacks made them sniper bait. Machine gunners were also targeted. Shoot them and the enemy has no heavy firepower. But the ultimate prize for any sniper was enemy snipers. Deal with them, and you have the enemy laid out before you, like a buffet, and you are spoilt for whom to shoot first.

"Listen up guys," bellowed Danny. "Make your way over to the main building in five minutes for orders. I'm sure Archie can squeeze in a quick shit, in that time." He winked at me, having not forgotten my transgression.

I grinned and took it on the chin. What does a man have to do to make amends? Word got around quickly that we only needed to take weapons with us, and to bring brews if we wanted, since we could be a while. Jamie was already putting the finishing touches to a couple of hot chocolates, when it was time to go over to the house. "Nice one matey," I thanked him, as I gratefully received a cup.

The whole Platoon made its way over to the house mob-handed. As we arrived, we were told to hang tight whilst

Dale organised who was to sit where. When delivering orders around an earth model, ideally you want the guys sat in their formations for the operation, so they can orientate themselves to the ground, and face the model in the direction they will be travelling. There was a bit of shuffling around, Dale putting bums on seats so to speak, whilst our OC Justin was putting the finishing touches to the notes in his hand. I noticed a few new faces in the audience; probably guys attached to the Company, such as mortar-fire controllers and artillery observers, anyone that put the cards in our favour when the shooting started. Before long, everyone was in position, and Dale commanded everyone to settle down. I noticed that names of features were now in place on the model, on large pieces of card so everyone could read them. He stood off to one side with a long stick, and handed the orders over to Justin.

"Thank you Sergeant Major," began Justin. "Gentlemen, you are about to receive orders for a deliberate silent Battalion night attack onto Mount Longdon." He paused to allow his bold statement to sink in. We were going in cold, dark, and as quiet as possible, in order to get on top of the enemy before they reacted. "Task organisation; B Company complete, attached to us are mortar fire controllers from our mortar platoon, artillery observers from

29th Commando Regiment Royal Artillery, naval gunfire observers from HMS Avenger, and engineers from 9 Squadron. Welcome." So that's who the new faces were.

Justin introduced the model at a deliberate pace, so everyone could take notes, Dale pointing out features with the stick. "North pointer to orientate you, here you have the area in general. We are here at Estancia House. These piles of spoil are as follows; our objective Longdon, and these are Wireless Ridge, Tumbledown, Harriet, Two Sisters, William, and Sapper Hill. The info on the cards speaks for itself. The chalk represents streams, and the string represents roads."

He briefly described the area, and our primary objective, Mount Longdon. There were small cardboard signs placed on sub-objectives named Wing Forward, Fly Half and Full Back, the Commanding Officer being a big rugby fan. Justin then proceeded to go into detail about the ground we would be operating en route to Longdon, and detail about the mountain itself.

Longdon was an imposing feature, 600 feet at its highest point, and dominated the surrounding moorland for quite some distance. The mountain consisted of a series of large rock runs that were steep at the western end, and petered off towards Wireless Ridge in the east. The model was formed in such a way that Longdon looked like a headless dinosaur skeleton partially dug up, with Wireless Ridge as its tail.

Justin then went into his 'situation' paragraph, going into detail about the bigger picture with regards to the campaign as it stood at the moment, and what effect our attack on Longdon would have on the enemy, in the grand scheme of things. To be honest, I felt a lot of it was well above my pay scale, but knowledge is power, so they say.

He went into detail about the enemy occupying Longdon; morale, strength, weapons, routine, and their patrol programme, which was virtually non-existent since the skirmish with our guys a few nights ago. He covered possible future intentions, likely arcs for their heavy machineguns, a possible fallback plan, minefields, killing areas, you name it.

The Patrols guys had really done their homework, night after night going forward to gather as much information for us as possible, so hopefully there were no surprises on the day of the race. In a nutshell, Justin explained that if we hit the enemy hard enough, they would fold, as proven at Goose Green. It was then that the whole magnitude of what we were about to embark on began to catch up with me. I could feel my stomach tighten with pre-match nerves, which had not been present since we were being soaked through on the landing craft, on the way to the beach in broad daylight. Things were suddenly very real; we could well be killing the enemy very shortly, or getting killed by them. I glanced around at some of the other guys. If they were in the same boat as me, they kept a good poker face, and weren't letting on.

Justin then went into detail about friendly forces, announcing that our Second Battalion was in reserve, should the opportunity arise to exploit success. He then gave us our mission statement. "B Company, your mission is to clear Fly Half and Full Back. Be prepared to support C Company when they attack Wireless Ridge, in order to clear the enemy from within the 3 PARA boundary." He paused, before repeating the mission statement. This was done so you are left in no doubt what you are there to do. Fly Half and Full Back was pretty much the whole feature that is Mount Longdon. Wing Forward was a task for A Company.

He then moved on to his 'execution' paragraph. "Guys, firstly we will deal with the prelim moves, prior to our advance to the start line. Straight after those orders, we will move up to the western base of Mount Vernet in assault order. Bergens will be left stacked in section lines just outside your trenches. We will march in slow time to

Mount Vernet, where my Command Group will move into over-watch of the objective, for any last-minute adjustment to my orders." Justin's Command Group consisted of his radio operator, all the platoon commanders and their radio operators, plus the attached group commanders. Should Justin want to fine tune his plan, he could inform the various commanders, who would pass what was relevant down to whoever needed to know. What I wasn't looking forward to was the pain in the arse march up the hill across them bastard rock fields, where you were just asking for a busted ankle.

"Once in position," Justin continued, "we will wait for the order from the Commanding Officer to begin our approach to this stream junction here." Dale pointed out the feature on the model. "Order of march will be 6 Platoon, then my group minus platoon commanders, then 5 Platoon, then the Sergeant Major's group, followed up by 4 Platoon."

Dale's Sergeant Major group would consist of himself, his radio op, Company medics, 4 Platoon's commander, and our Company Clerk, who would assume the role of ammo donkey and runner. 4 Platoon's commander would react on Dale's orders from Justin, and deploy his platoon forward, should there be a need for it.

"We will stop short of the stream junction," explained Justin, as Dale traced the route with his stick, "and we will meet up with a team from Patrols, who will guide us into the start line prior to our attack. Once in position, 4 Platoon left, 5 in the centre and 6 on the right, advancing on a broad front, you must be aware that we will have A Company to our left, clearing Wing Forward, and Patrols to our right, who will prevent any enemy reinforcements from Tumbledown, and also keep eyes on Wireless Ridge. C Company will be behind us in reserve, ready to move through us onto Wireless Ridge, when we have cleared the main feature."

He asked for any questions. There were none from anyone; I think everyone had the same dreaded feeling as me now, since I noticed a few of the audience looking rather uneasy. The plan sounded straightforward. I think it was the fact that it was for real, no more training. He then talked through a series of 'actions on' measures, should anything happen that could cock up the whole mission; people getting injured en-route, people getting lost, enemy seeing us before we get sorted out at the start line, etc, etc.

He handed the floor over to Dale, who delivered the 'service support' paragraph. It was a sergeant major's bag. He went into detail with regards to casualty procedure, prisoner handling, what he wanted certain people to carry in their gear and where, ammo resupply, anything that involved administration for the coming operation. He went to town, and I noticed all the corporals and sergeants scribbling like mad into their notebooks.

He allowed pens to cool before he then went to town on random people, in the form of questioning them on what he had told them. If they got it wrong, he didn't bollock them, he patiently re-issued the information. It was important that everyone, not just commanders, knew what he wanted and when it was to be done, as it could involve taking or saving lives.

Justin took over again, thanking Dale for his method of getting the message across. Justin's last part of the orders was 'command and signals', which was very much the business of whom was to assume command, should anyone be taken out of the fight for whatever reason, and what radio frequencies we needed to be on for the operation, etc. He asked the artillery observer, who would be in charge of our artillery support, for a time check. The observer, a captain, announced what the time would be in two minutes time, and this prompted all watch wearers, especially commanders, to prepare their own watches for the countdown to the time stated by him.

Once watches were set, Justin was back in the driver's seat. "In summary, guys, we are going to take Longdon and those fuckers sat on it. Stanley is just twelve miles away, and I'm pissed off with being cold, wet and tired, longer than I have to be. I'm sure you will agree." The lads broke into a muffled cheer; he raised a hand to calm it down. "Guys, make no mistake, by what we've heard about Goose Green, we won't have it all our own way. Just trust your commanders, and do your job. If all else fails, make your way to the top of Longdon, understood?" We all nodded. This was it. "Right then," he concluded, "get your shit squared. My Command group will take the lead to Vernet in an hour, see you there."

We all began to disperse. Amid the hustle and bustle, a few of the lads cast their eye over the model for a few minutes, just to get the lay of the land in their heads. Jamie and I quickly made our way back to our position to do some last-minute kit adjustments. The cold fog began to lift, and you could now see the whole settlement was a hive of activity. To the east of the settlement, I could see one of the companies, don't know which one, making its way in two columns up the long gradient towards Mount Estancia.

"Kit on and stack your Bergens," shouted Danny, and I went through the same routine of placing my kit on. Quilted suit packed away, webbing on, belts of ammo wrapped around my torso, barrel bag on, and helmet on. A few of the lads were sat once again outside their trenches, smoking or picking their noses, enjoying the calm before the impending storm. I was getting nervous, make no mistake, but I was comfortable in knowing I wasn't the only one.

Jamie looked over to me. "Things are going to get real tasty soon, my man." If that was his attempt at comforting me, it wasn't working. He was worried, he must be, and I defy anyone who was not nervous about the coming operation. I knew it was pre-match nerves, but I now started to question what I'd let myself in for. This clearly was a case of me joining the Army for a world of adventure, and it was now cashing in on my obligation to the country. Was the way I was feeling what them poor sods felt in the trenches, just before going over the top at the Somme? Or them guys just about to jump into Normandy? It must be. The fact was it was my generation's turn to fight, plain and simple. Now man up, Archie, you fucking dick.

"Prepare to move," was the order called down the line, and with that we clambered to our feet. A bit of jumping up and down and shifting of kit to get comfy, usual stuff, but

I'd given up trying to get boxer shorts out of the crack of my arse, as I had too much kit on.

We started to move slowly towards the eastern side of the settlement, and we slowly fell into column, beginning our march up to Mount Vernet. We crossed a small road bridge as we came out of Estancia, turned left and headed northeast, uphill towards the many rock fields that surrounded Vernet. The pace was very slow when the lead elements started to pick their way around the worst of the rock fields. I liked to think Justin wanted to keep injuries to a minimum on the way to our objective. A few of the rock traverses were a bit technical and slippery, but we managed to stay on our feet, as we picked our way slowly towards our concentration area. I was sweating like a lunatic, no change there, but I was past caring about that. I kept glancing right, hoping to catch a glimpse of Longdon, but Justin's route ensured we were out of sight of the objective; probably something to do with it being covered in enemy was a good bet.

After a couple of hours of rock balancing, slipping and sliding, we got into our concentration area on the western side of Vernet. Justin then took all those in his Command Group further up the feature, to get eyes on the objective. We just sat tight and got comfortable, with the quilted suit display team deploying in record time. I hoped we were not staying long. I would not want to try and sleep, with bits of rock sticking out of the ground everywhere, and I couldn't see any flat smooth ground anywhere. Accommodation-wise, we clearly had it too good at Teal and Estancia, despite the cold.

Jamie got a brew on the go, and I could smell the aroma of cigarettes drifting across our position. It was now a case of sitting tight, until the order came to move out towards our rendezvous with our Patrol guides. I was sure it was getting colder. I took my leather gloves off so I could sort out my boot laces, and by the time I had my gloves back on, my hands were in pain. After a little while, my hands returned back to their usual state. Apart from drinking tea, picking our noses and putting cam cream on, there wasn't much else to do until the Boss got back from Justin's Command Group. There might be slight changes to the plan, but I doubted it. I'm no expert tactician by any stretch of the imagination, but what Justin gave in his orders was straightforward enough for us Private soldiers to understand. And that's the point. If it's all going wrong, every man, whatever their rank, needs to know what needs to be achieved. In training, we were forever being told to pay attention to the plan; you are only one bullet away from being in charge.

Tony came back from Command Group. No change to the orders, the plan was set. B Company was the lead company to the rendezvous with Patrols, which would ensure we would be in the right order of march, for Patrols to guide us to our start line. We were starting to lose light now, and it wouldn't be long before it got dark. Justin and Dale were doing the rounds, chatting to every single one of us and shaking our hands, as well as cracking the odd joke. They came over to where me and Jamie were sat, and we clambered to our feet to greet them.

"Alright lads?" Justin enquired.

"Yes sir," I replied.

"Archie, what's on your mind, mate?" asked Dale.

I just shook my head and let out a low whistle. "This is the real deal, isn't it?"

"Yep, pretty much," Justin replied. "Doesn't mean you have to like it, me neither."

Dale placed his hand on my shoulder. "You'll be fine, remember, and just make your way to the top."

"No problems Sir."

Dale looked over to Jamie. "You OK?"

133

"I'm fine, thanks sir, how are you?"

"OK." Dale grinned. "OK."

They shook our hands and moved on to the next group of lads, sitting amongst the rocks. We sat down and I rummaged through my smock pockets for some chocolate. I broke it open and offered Jamie some; he waved his hand in refusal. Not like him. "You OK, mate?" I asked in a low voice.

"Not really, Archie, I'm shitting myself."

Now it was my turn to comfort him. "So am I. We all are. Didn't you see Justin and Dale? This is their first fight too, and we are all in the same boat, mate."

He grinned and nodded. "You're right."

"Mount up," shouted Dale. Jamie and I struggled to our feet again, got our gear comfortable and shook hands. The light was fading fast. I just wished the bloody shit weather would fade with it. No such luck, in fact change that. I'll keep the weather in exchange for no Argentinians on our objective. If only. We stood around waiting for 4 Platoon to head off over the rise towards our rendezvous, shortly followed by Justin's group. By the time we moved out, it was as good as dark. We were on.

CHAPTER 7: The Foot of the Mountain

The full moon breaking through the dispersing clouds made our picking through the rock fields easier, as we could see where we were placing our feet. The cold night air was no less savage. Large vapour clouds marked the positions of almost everyone, as we picked our way through, sweating under our combat loads. Most of us gunners still had our machineguns on our shoulders, since this helped us keep balance, as we clambered over the more technical parts of these rivers of rock. As much as we tried, remaining totally silent on our approach was almost impossible. The scraping of boots on jagged rock, and the odd clatter of belt ammunition wrapped around a soldier's torso were quite prominent in the night air. Some of my nervousness had faded, since the time for thinking was over, and we were getting on with what we received a salary for.

After what felt like an eternity, we started to clear the rock fields. As we descended, forward left of our column was a large cluster of reflective surfaces. As we slowly passed on their right side, it became clear to me that they were ponds of standing water, nothing more. We began to veer left, following a small trickling stream on our right side, with the ponds on our left. The soggy ground began to suck at our boots, with the odd rock to trip you up thrown in for good measure. We continued to follow the stream for some time, until the column ground to a halt. Up ahead, I noticed people beginning to kneel down, taking up alternate arcs, facing left and right of our column. I got to face right, not that there was very much to look at. On the other side of the stream, the ground climbed gradually. It appeared to be flat at the top, not much up there.

I looked left and could see a figure moving slowly down the line. As the figure drew close, I could make out John's profile. "We are just short of the rendezvous," he whispered. "Patrols will then guide us to our start line, OK?" Those who could hear him nodded, including me, and he moved back to his place in the line. Unlike our other marches across the island, there was no aroma of cigarettes or hexamine blocks. It was full-on tactical, talking and noise to a minimum.

It wasn't long before the column began to get to its feet, and start shuffling forward again. I'd changed from having the Gimpy across a shoulder. It was now slung across my front, ready for action. We were right on the enemy's doorstep now. We slowly made our way forward. The stream started to get wider and noisier, with more water trickling through it. With the full moon and clear sky, the surrounding moorland was very well-lit, and the shadows cast by random outcrops of rock made the whole venture even creepier.

We eventually arrived at what appeared to be a busy stream junction. Patrols Company was there in force, both providing protection for the rendezvous, plus also picking up their respective companies, to guide them to their start lines. As we made our way closer to Patrols, I could make out soldiers stood in the stream. Fuck that, talk about making your bollocks shrink. Our progress was almost at a snail's pace now, and it wasn't long before I could see why. The guys in the water, who turned out to be Royal Engineers attached to us, had laid on a series of ladders and planks of wood, to get us across the stream with our heavy loads. God bless 'em. They were stood in the stream making sure we stayed dry. Nice one, lads.

When it came to my turn to cross, I had to traverse a ladder, and the engineers each side of me basically grabbed my arms without ceremony, and whispered instructions to me as I placed my feet on the ladder rungs, almost like a parent talking a toddler through their first steps. As I got to the other side, they let go and gave me the thumbs up. We may have been the combat troops, but this was sure as shit their crossing site. You danced to their tune. They didn't care what rank you were, or what your status was in your unit. You all got the same treatment, and rightly so. We slowly filed on, making room for the other lads crossing, and then stopped to take a knee, to allow for the remainder of the Company to cross.

Sometime later, after freezing our tits off, I noticed Dale make his way up the line to the front of the column. This clearly meant the Company was now complete again, since the Company Sergeant Major would normally be at the back of the line. Before long, we got to our feet and began to move forward again, and as we shuffled on, we passed Dale, who was counting us through, one of his many duties in battle, making sure we hadn't lost anyone, through injury or just plain lost.

We started to move right, away from the stream bank, but hugging into the gradient on our right, so not to expose us to Longdon as much as possible. We continued on this course for some time, until our cover on the right began to reduce, and there was nothing but open ground. There was Mount Longdon to our forward right, huge and looming, and to be honest, very intimidating. The model didn't lie; it did look like dinosaur remains, huge sheets of rock sticking out of the mountain, like a huge ribcage. That dreaded feeling had now returned. To me, it felt like every Argentine soldier on that mountain was just sat there looking at our column, waiting for the right time to ambush us.

Our column moved around to the right, and began to slowly make its way up the valley that took us directly in front of the mountain. With every couple of steps, I kept peering left, because I felt so exposed in our current position. Surely their sentries must have seen us by now. Please be asleep? I was hoping they had got up and fucked off back into Stanley for a pint, anything that would have this night pass without incident.

After a short period of time, we began to pass soldiers on our left. They were kneeling and lying down, facing Longdon. 4 Platoon were now at their start line, it was our turn next. The Patrols guys had actually placed white strips of tape down, to mark where every sub-unit was going to form up. This clearly said to me that Patrols had been there before, taking their chances with the enemy sentries. Truly remarkable, these guys were without doubt experts in their craft.

We began to get placed into our respective positions. This part of the operation remained in the hands of Patrols Company. They had Private soldiers, who were to be fair, above average intelligence, switched on operators placing companies of men into position for the up-and-coming battle, a task not to be taken lightly. In front of me in the line was Zane. He was basically being put exactly where the Patrols guys wanted him to lay, no ifs or buts. Then it was mine and Jamie's turn, since we worked as a pair, a gun team, me as the gunner and Jamie helping me manage the gun and also feed the thing. A Patrols guy walked over to me, took me gently by the arm, and led me to the spot where he wanted me. I un-slung the gun, slowly deploying its bipod legs, to avoid them springing open with a clatter. I lay down in the grass, which was just about long enough to cover my barrel muzzle. Our guide then lay down to my right, almost on top of me, and gave me a thumbs-down gesture, which was the NATO sign for enemy. Then in a karate chop motion, he pointed his arm in the direction of Longdon. I nodded. He gave me a gentle dig in the shoulder, and then got up and placed Jamie next to me, carrying out the same ritual for his benefit. The Patrols guy got to his feet, and went to fetch the next guy in line. I looked at Jamie, who just pulled a face and winked at me, forever the comedian.

The moon made Longdon very prominent in the darkness. From our position, the right side of the mountain looked like a large saddle feature, with huge rock faces at each end. To the left were a series of jagged rock runs, which looked all the more sinister with huge shadows cast by the moon. I looked left and right of our start line. Small columns of breath vapour marked where the guys had been placed. The wind picked up slightly, making my shivering all the more intense. I could hear a series of clicks to my left. As it grew louder, it very quickly dawned on me what they were, and my stomach turned over. Bayonets were being fitted. I tried my hardest not to vomit. I managed to keep it in my mouth and force it down again, burning my throat. This shit wasn't funny anymore. I looked at Jamie, waiting for him to fit his bayonet, but he slowly shook his head. Maybe he felt fighting as a gun team would only be made more difficult, if a bayonet was being swung around whilst helping me. I looked to the left and saw people getting to their feet, and starting to move forward. I clambered to my feet and tried to remain calm as I stowed the bipod legs. I looked left and right. The whole Company was on its feet moving forward.

The ground rose gently, and care had to be taken not to trip on rocks, hidden in the ankle-deep frozen grass that crunched under our feet. Progress was slow and steady; Longdon loomed overhead, but didn't appear to get any closer. The gradient began to rise more prominently now, making me breathe heavier. We were just short of the first series of large rocks that rose above us.

Then there was a loud thud to our rear left, followed by a loud scream. I could hear people calling 'man down' and 'medic'. 4 Platoon? I didn't know. We all went to ground; I was on my belly in record time with Jamie crawling in next

141

to me, on my left. We scanned the ground ahead. There was a lot of commotion coming from 4 Platoon by the sound of things, not good. I started to hear chatter and shouting to my front. I couldn't make out what it was, but it quickly dawned on me that it wasn't us. There was a pop, a whoosh and a plume of smoke from a cluster of rocks above us, and another pop above as our entire position was lit up by a flare. The shouting in the rocks above us got all the more excitable. They see us, they can fucking see us!

Green and orange tracer began to stream down to our left, since it was 4 Platoon that was making a lot of noise initially. But then enemy fire shifted to us. Rounds were thumping into the ground around our position. Sparks flew as they smashed into rock hidden in the grass. I could see a series of muzzle flashes from amongst the rocks above us, so I cocked the gun, and began to fire short bursts at the flashes. All this seemed to do was attract their attention, and green and orange tracer then smashed and thudded all around us, fuck!

"Move forward, move forward, get to some cover," someone shouted. No one moved, the flares had us caught like rabbits in headlights.

"Fucking move," shouted Danny.

We got up mob-handed and dashed forward. Grabbing the gun by the carry handle, I legged it to the first cluster of rocks I could hide behind. Just as the light faded from one flare, another took its place, we were caught in the open and we had to get in amongst the rocks. Jamie was right on my tail as we slid in behind some decent cover. I tried to site the gun in a decent position with the legs down, but I was too exposed, as tracer smashed into our cover. Legs up, lower profile. As I tried to get into position, our rocks got hit with incoming fire. Jamie leaned out to his left and snapped off a few shots with his SLR, but then ducked back in, just as rounds smashed into our cover again.

Pinned down, another flare lit up our position. I could see all order of formation had gone out of the window. The guys were literally behind cover in various sized groups, just trying to get the upper hand. We had a fair idea which muzzle flash above us was giving us trouble, and some of the lads were giving it back, as I could see red tracer splashing all over their position. For a little while, the enemy position would be silent, but would start up again, maybe with a new gunner. The din around us was tremendous; machine gun fire, screaming, shouting, you name it.

I took my barrel bag off, as the strap was really chafing my neck. Jamie then grabbed my arm and pointed to the left. I could make out John shouting at me, but amongst the noise I couldn't make out what he wanted. It became apparent, when everyone dashed out of cover and took a leap forward. I quickly grabbed the gun, as Jamie had already begun sprinting ahead.

As I legged it after him, I noticed him jump over a small group of rocks. As I got closer to him, green and orange tracer began to thud and smash into the ground, just right of me. I went for the rocks. I then tripped, and got a face full of timber and peat as I fell to the floor. I was winded as I landed on the gun, my face killing me. I rolled over, and propped myself against a peat wall of sorts. The floor then started shouting Spanish at me, and as I scrambled for my weapon, it became more animated. A drifting flare above lit up what appeared to be a face. I fired, and this face shattered like an egg, showering the floor and me in brain, skull, teeth and blood. The gunfire rendered me deaf and my ears rang. Out of the darkness, another face and a pair of hands appeared and lunged at me, grabbing my throat and face. I grabbed at the wrists and attempted to prise them away.

"Jamie, Jamie," I screamed, muffled because my ears were still ringing. The guy engaging me was screaming also. Didn't have a clue what he wanted, probably help, the same as me. "Jamie, Jamie, help me," I begged.

I managed to get my right boot into the guy's stomach area and pushed, whilst using my gloved hands to squeeze his wrists as hard as I could, which loosened his grasp. I managed to overpower him, and pin him to the floor. Still in control of his hands, I head-butted him again and again.

"You fuck, fuck you," I shouted, spitting in his face. He screamed out for help. I smashed my head into his face again. "Fuck you, you fucking fuck," I roared.

I ploughed my head into his bare face until he was silent. I let go of his wrists, and his arms flopped to the floor. I scrambled back against a wall of rocks. Soaked with sweat, I caught my breath, and in the drifting light of the flares searched for my weapon.

I saw in the fading light that the Gimpy was underneath the legs of my sparring partner. I crawled over and grabbed his right leg, and swung it over his left. I pulled at the weapon, but it was still caught under his bodyweight. I grabbed the right side of his duvet jacket and gave an almighty heave, and rolled him onto his front, freeing up the gun. I grabbed it with both hands and scrambled back to the end of his trench. I clutched the gun tightly in my arms and rested my head against the trench wall. The ringing in my ears began to fade. The violent din outside returned in full force. I could hear rounds snapping overhead, rounds smashing off rock, thudding into peat. Men were screaming, swearing and crying.

I had to rejoin my platoon. As I leant forward to get to my feet, pain exploded through my head, as something hot and solid punched into the left side of my face, pinning me to the trench wall. A bright red glow blinded me. "Who the fuck are you?" growled a voice, clearly English.

"Archie, Archie," I panicked, "5 Platoon." The solid object was released from the side of my face, and the red glow disappeared instantly. My night vision was ruined. The trench was now full of red drifting blobs, as I tried to focus again in the dark.

"You've made a right mess of these guys," said the voice. "Can you walk?" I nodded, and a hand grabbed hold of my webbing strap, and yanked me out of the trench. I clutched the gun even tighter, so as not to drop it. I was forced onto my back; my helper placed a knee gently on my chest and began talking. "Yeah, Roger that. I've got one of yours here. Show red light. Make yourself known to me." As I regained focus, I realised my helper was none other than Dale. He must have heard me, and come to investigate. Chaos reigned all around us, and he was knelt up, pinning me underneath him, trying to get me back to my platoon.

"Show red light," he repeated, "over." A few seconds passed. "Yep, seen, I'm coming to you. Sit tight." He looked back down to me. "You OK?"

"Yes sir."

"Good, sort your weapon out, I'm taking you to meet up with 5 again, understand?"

He released me and I rolled onto my front, and made sure the gun was still in working order; belt untwisted, barrel still on, done. "Ready," I called out above the gunfire.

"OK," he said, "let's go." He pulled me to my feet, and pushed me away from the trench. As I peered back, he threw a grenade into the trench and ran past me. There was a loud thud, and a huge plume of white phosphorous smoke billowed out of the hole. I picked up the pace and caught up with him, as he sought refuge behind some rocks with some other guys. We looked back, as green and orange tracer splashed all over the burning trench. The enemy above wasn't taking any chances, and were hosing anything that moved below them.

A hand grabbed my shoulder. In the drifting light of flares, I could make out Zane talking to Dale, and we were back with 5 Platoon. Dale turned to me. "Here you go, Archie boy. No more hero stuff, OK?"

I nodded, and then Zane pulled me over to him, and shouted in my ear. "Right then, we've cleared some of the bunkers, but this fuck up front is holding the Company up." He peered around our cover and pointed up the hill. I leaned out behind him, and saw an offending machinegun post. We leant back in. "He's chewed up the platoon pretty bad," reported Zane. "Danny, John and a couple of the guys are forward now, trying to knock him out. 6 Platoon are trying to come around on the right side, but they have problems of their own. 4 Platoon are trying to get into the rock runs to our left. These fucks have got their shit sited proper, know what I mean?" I nodded. I think he was trying to tell me that we were not having it all our own way. The problem position was just below the skyline of the saddle, and until we dealt with it, we were not going anywhere.

Then a series of grenades thudded all over the machinegun post. We leant out of cover to observe. The position was smouldering, and there were a couple of our guys milling about in front of it. As a flare burst overhead, the whole mountainside was drowned in a brilliant white light. The two guys in front of the knocked-out bunker were instantly splashed in green tracer. One burst into a cloud of white phosphorous smoke. The incoming fire must have hit his grenades. The other was hit with numerous rounds, which took his face and bits of his torso off. His body ended up in a sitting position, against the front of the bunker. The horror show ended as the flare light faded out. Zane looked at me. "I hope they weren't our guys."

Another flare burst into life above us, and we looked at the body sat in front of the bunker. As the flare drifted and the shadows moved, it looked like the body was moving. Then another burst of green and orange splashed all over it. More pieces flicked off, but the body stayed sat up. The fucker still firing at it was forward right of us, and as the flare light faded out, I could make out some of our guys scrambling around to the right to deal with it. In the darkness, there was a loud thud, as a grenade went into the enemy firer's bunker, followed by a series of screams from inside, which lasted what seemed like ages. Two rifle shots brought the screaming to a close, position taken.

Slowly, and quite rightly cautiously, we broke cover and made our way up towards the saddle. As we drew close to where the two guys were shot up, it was clearly evident they were our guys. We made a wide berth around the figure smouldering in white phosphorous, fearing his remaining ammo might cook off in the heat. The guy sat in front of the smouldering bunker was plain to see. Jaw shot away, helmet caved in on one side, his left arm almost severed. As we picked our way past the bunker itself, you couldn't help noticing the aroma of human shit coming from it. Did the occupants defecate in the bunker? Or did their bowels get ripped open when they were smashed with grenades? Who knows? Who cares? Position clear.

CHAPTER 8: The Ascent

Word came round to sit tight, before we committed ourselves over the saddle. The enemy were full of surprises tonight, and their concealment of bunkers was excellent. They wouldn't open fire until you were right on top of them, which made for very grim fighting. More of our guys were making their way up behind us. These guys were gun and MILAN teams, stopping short with us before we went over the top.

I looked over to the right side of the saddle. In the low light, a figure was making his way through the rocks towards me, jingling and rattling as he walked. As he pulled up next to me, I saw it was Jamie. He was draped in shitloads of belt ammo. "Hello stranger," he called out, as he stripped off his load, "where have you been?"

I didn't want to talk about the trench I fell in. "Got caught up on some wire. Dale helped me get loose."

"Man," Jamie said, shaking his head, "this is some crazy shit." I nodded. We tucked into some rocks, as more flares burst overhead. As the flares drifted across the mountain, it was clearly evident what the Company had been through, up to this point. There were a series of smouldering bunkers. Bodies, both theirs and ours, were left as they fell, some in grotesque positions. Nothing like what Hollywood would have you believe. But our part of the mountain was relatively quiet now. 4 and 6 Platoon were having a right time of it; grenades thudding in bunkers, people shouting and screaming, rounds pinging and smashing off rocks, quite a soundtrack.

"Listen up." It was Davo. "4 Platoon are getting chewed up bad, trying to get into the rock runs. My section is going to backtrack the way we came, and reinforce their push up the mountain. The remainder of the platoon are going to push over the saddle shortly, and provide close protection for these gun and MILAN teams, everyone clear?" Where was John, Danny, Boss? There were muffled replies and nodding heads. "Right then," Davo continued, "my section, grab your shit, let's go."

We made our way back down, the way we had come to the base of the saddle, using the flare light to our advantage, making our progress through the rocks and burning bunkers easier. Almost at the base of the feature, we skirted around to the right, which would lead us to 4 Platoon at the base of the rock runs. We stopped short, Davo getting on the radio, to let 4 Platoon know we were coming. I didn't fancy getting shot up by my own side. We took cover in a cluster of rocks and waited. In the flare light, I took a look at who was still with us; Davo, me, Jamie, Zane, Leighton. Shit, was that it? They can't be all dead, surely? I was not looking forward to joining 4 Platoon. Just on the other side of a huge slab of rock that separated us, they were in a full-on brawl with an enemy that was not having any of it.

Davo got to his feet. "Let's go, guys." We scrambled after him, and we slowly made our way around a large rock, and were greeted by what looked like a pile of logs. Next to the logs was a figure kneeling down, with a radio on his back. The soldier was talking into a handset. "What do you mean, anti-tank gun?" Davo tried to get his attention, to no avail. "Who?" the operator continued, "they have? Where? I need more information than that, have they got an anti-tank gun or not?" He looked around and got the fright of his life. Us bunch of menacing goons were peering at him through the darkness. He held his hand up to us, and spoke back into the handset. "Right, get off the skyline, and stay alert for those fucks still alive above you, got it? Out."

He turned to us. "Alright lads, please tell me your platoon is making better progress than us. We are getting the shit kicked out of us. We've got two alleyways of rock to clear, and they are dug in tight. These fucks aren't giving up ground for shit, let me show you." He led us further around the rock, to a point where we could see what he meant by alleyways. Huge slabs of rock that could almost pass for

153

prison walls, they were that high, with the enemy perched all over them, firing down at 4 Platoon. The alleys were also made hard going by the fact that they were uphill. This part of the objective looked like a bastard to clear out.

We went back to our previous position by the pile of logs. A flare burst above us, and revealed the pile of logs for what it actually was; these logs were wearing camouflage clothing. They were 4 Platoon dead. I turned away, trying to force down the vomit that was flooding my mouth, too late. I stepped away from the group, and sprayed the grass and my boots with the contents of my stomach. The burning throughout my core was intense.

I felt a hand on my shoulder, as I tried to calm down my retching. "You OK, matey?" I looked up and Davo was grinning at me, and gave me a friendly wink. "Yeah, sorry," he said. "Not what they show you in the brochure." The bodies were covered with a poncho, which covered the grimness of their demise. But seeing their legs and boots stacked up like firewood was just too much for me, reminded me of old pictures of Stalingrad or Auschwitz, you see in the history books.

Their platoon sergeant talked to me. "I couldn't leave 'em in the open," he stated, "getting shredded over and over again by grenades and incoming. My reserve section

154

played undertaker. Not nice, not nice at all. Our boss will be down in a minute. He's at the top of an alley, near the summit. He will be glad to see his new reserve section, thanks for volunteering."

In the alleyways, the hits just kept on coming. While we waited for 4 Platoon's boss to come down, we listened to the carnage unfolding above us. The gun and MILAN teams were now committed, and you could hear a horrendous amount of firepower going downrange. There were huge explosions rocking the backside of Longdon. Not too sure who was dishing it out, but it was intense. I hoped the guys up on the saddle were OK. We'd taken a mauling getting up there. I just hoped they could hold it. The flares above us continued to fade out, and instantly be replaced by fresh ones. As they drifted across the mountain, they revealed more of our grim surroundings. The pile of 4 Platoon dead, bloody bandages, empty ammo containers, brass cases from heavy gunfights, all the debris you expect from such a fight. In the flare light, we could see people coming out of an alley. A couple kept their eyes peeled at the top of the rocks, others carrying wounded personnel. As they got closer to us, we could see the wounded were badly mauled by the night's efforts. Their platoon sergeant called them over, and the wounded were put behind cover, a little distance from their dead friends. Their medics, who had been with them in the assault up the alley, looked in no better shape, but went about their duties, getting the guys patched up as best they could.

A soldier walked over to us, and outstretched his hand. "Thanks for coming down to help us out. I'm Jay, OC 4 Platoon."

Davo accepted his hand. "Hello sir, crazy shit we are in, yes?"

Jay nodded. "I've got a section holding the top of that alley, but at this time not committed to the summit. They've got some heavy shit up there, keeping us pinned in. Up on the cliff to our right, someone is rolling grenades in, hence our current condition. 5 Platoon are slowly dealing with them, and trying to protect the gun teams at the same time, as they are very exposed. The enemy has some kind of flak gun up there, and some kind of anti-tank weapon. Our artillery is trying to knock them out as we speak. Christ knows what's happened to this naval gunfire we are meant to have." We all just looked at each other. "Justin and Dale are with 6 Platoon," continued Jay, "trying to get them forward, but we've walked straight into the lion's den here, a very strong defensive screen." No shit, the dead and wounded were rising in number. "We need to get back up there, and deal with them fuckers up on the cliff, all set?"

We were ready to go, let's get this thing done. Jay set off at a patrol pace, followed by us in single file. We kept to the left side of the alley as we began to climb. One couldn't help but to keep peering up at the right side, looking for potential targets. We got about halfway up, when some small rocks up to the right gave way. All of us swung our barrel muzzles up there instinctively. The rocks clattered down the wall, and one of them exploded.

There was an almighty thud, and the right side of my face stung, like someone had given it a right proper slap. My ears exploded into a high-pitched ring. I fell onto my hands and knees, and as I looked up, I could see Jay and Davo, firing like mad up the alley. The ringing in my head drowned out any soundtrack of battle. They dived to the floor, and I copied them, as the ground vibrated with another big thud. I stayed put, with my face planted in the peat. I felt the ground thud underneath me a few more times. We were all going to die.

I felt a hand roughly grab my right shoulder and flip me over. Davo knocked me across the same side of the face that still stung like a bastard. Slowly the soundtrack of combat returned to me in full force. "You OK?" he called out. "Can you walk?"

I couldn't feel anything wrong with me, apart from being broadsided with the ultimate hangover. "Yeah, did we get 'em?"

"I'm not sure. 5 Platoon are going to have to clear 'em out, before we try and push up again."

Davo and Jamie pulled me to my feet, and we made our way back down to the rendezvous point at the bottom of the alley. "You're not having much luck tonight, are you?" said Jamie. He wasn't wrong, but I'd rather be a bit battered than dead, wrapped in a poncho. He led me to where the 4 Platoon wounded were sat.

Straightaway, one of their medics tended to me. With a red torch light, he examined the side of my face. "I don't think you've got anything to worry about, mate," he stated. "I think you just got pebble-dashed. I would give you pain relief, but I think I'm going to need it later."

Fair cop. Relief washed through me. By the sound of things, the grenade did nothing more than ring my bell for me. I fished out one of my water bottles, and took several greedy gulps. Despite the intense cold of the night air, the cold water was refreshing. I took time to take in my surroundings. Off to my left, down near our start line, I could just make out a load of dark shapes, slowly making their way towards us. I stood up and gingerly made my way to where those still fit to fight had gathered. I pointed in the direction of the slow-moving shapes. "Look out there, can you see 'em?"

"A Company," announced Jay. "They were meant to clear the open spur to our north, but they've been getting a lot of harassing fire from snipers and mortars, by what is being said over the radio." By the look of things, they were attempting to seek refuge behind the mountain, since their objective appeared to be untenable, and they were unable to remain on for a long period of time. Up above us, we heard the thud of grenades at the top of the alleys, followed by some God-awful screaming which continued for some time. I looked at Jay. "Your 5 Platoon are taking care of things for us," he said to the remainder of my section. "Get ready to move."

After a short while, fresh screams could still be heard, but no more grenades. At one point, there was someone up there begging to be spared, and then another scream that went right through you. The scream became a muffled gargle, which after a while faded into silence. The grim purpose of the bayonet was being employed by 5 Platoon guys. I shuddered at the thought of such business. 5

Platoon had taken a mauling getting up to the summit, and their good-manners guide had long since been ditched in a burning bunker or two. There comes a point in a battle when you just need to get the grim and unthinkable done, such is the job description for a soldier.

Jay began to lead us back up our alley, once again keeping our eyes peeled high right, as we climbed to join the remainder of 4 Platoon at the top. As we got near them, I could see red, orange and green tracer streaming past from right to left, which didn't make any sense. But after thinking it over, it made perfect sense. Our gun teams must be using enemy ammunition, and after all, the enemy did have the same weapon systems as us, give or take some minor alterations. The gun teams were dishing it out in spades to whoever was on the eastern end of Longdon. MILAN missiles went roaring downrange to their targets. The din was incredible. All of a sudden, there was a streak of white light from the back end of Longdon, and an almighty boom off to our right, our fire-support base rendered silent. We heard a muffled voice on Jay's radio handset. "Yeah, Roger that," replied Jay. "What's the damage?" There was another muffled response. "Roger," Jay said, "let me know if there is anything we can do. Friendlies will be passing through us soon, out."

We all looked at him for an update. He turned to address us. "The anti-tank gun we've been trying to knock out has just destroyed a MILAN team complete." One of the lads gave out a low whistle. "The fire-support base is in bad shape," reported Jay. "The OC is on the hill with your 5 Platoon now, plus his artillery observer. They're trying to deal with it. A Company will be passing through us shortly, to deal with the main defensive position, and we will become fire-support. When we get the word, we are going to crawl out of this fucking alley, and we will start engaging the positions as we spot them, understood?"

We nodded. I looked back down the alley, and a large group of what could only be A Company was gathering.

CHAPTER 9: The Summit

All sense of time had been lost, as far as I was concerned. We'd been in action for several hours. In that space of time, we as a Company had been badly mauled, by the look of things. Back at Estancia, we were probably a bit too cocksure about the quality of the Argentine soldier. So far, by what I had experienced and witnessed, these guys were no pushover by any stretch of the imagination. Varying in quality, let it be said, but none of them made it easy for us. Our mission as a Company was to capture the main feature on the summit, but we had just about cleared the western side of the mountain. Now A Company, though not as planned, were about to push through our positions and finish the job. B Company shouldn't feel inferior. We soaked up a lot of punishment, and the guys wrapped in a poncho at the bottom of the rock runs were testament to that, never mind the wounded.

Sat at the top of our alley, we watched some of A Company move up, just short of us. Jay made his way down to them. Our gun teams already on the summit spluttered back into action, after getting royally pasted by the anti-tank gun. Red, orange and green tracer streamed across the back end of Longdon, at enemies hidden in the darkness. Give it to 'em guys, and fuck them up.

162

Jay moved back up to us. "Right then, scores on the doors." He had our attention. "In a minute, we are going to push forward out of here, and get eyes on their main position. By what the A Company lads have said, it's in a bowl of sorts on the summit, which drops down and away to the north. 1 Platoon are going to join us as a fire-base, and 2 Platoon is going to push around the left side of the alleys, and start to clear them out. 3 Platoon will be in reserve at the bottom of this alley." He paused, as a series of loud explosions rocked the back end of the mountain. With a bit of luck, that fucking anti-tank gun had been dealt with now. Once the bombardment eased off, he continued. "5 and 6 are going to start pushing forward, level with the bowl, to draw fire away from the static and exposed gun teams. Once the main position has been secured, we as a Company will move back the way we came, to a RAP being set up as we speak, near the bottom of the rock runs, OK?" We all nodded. The Regimental Aid Post, which is run by the Regimental Sergeant Major, is a location for dead and wounded to be collected from both sides, and a prisoner holding area.

Jay moved up to the top of the alley, and began to move in a crouch to avoid being seen, to a position where we could set up to support A Company. He moved about for some time, probably checking out alternative positions, should we become the focus of the enemy's fury. He then scampered back to us. "Let's go, keep low."

We set off after him, going firm only when the flares burst above us. Noise was not the issue, just being seen. The noise around us remained horrendous. As the flares faded out, we scampered forward, towards the jagged teeth-like rocks that marked the top of the bowl. He sited us one at a time, pointing out likely enemy bunkers. The enemy had proven they were not in the habit of showing their cards too soon. These fuckers remained silent for now. Jamie crawled in besides me, rattling like mad, since he was still draped in hundreds of rounds of belt ammo for me to use. After the initial contact when the battle started, we were back together. Such is the craziness of these situations. He winked at me. "Let's give it to these fucks, Archie boy. You shoot, and I feed."

We clashed helmets together; we were on the same page for this one. Just rear left of us, 1 Platoon were on their hands and knees, scampering into position. As another flare burst above the far end of the bowl, little could be seen in the shadows of the rocks that gave away any sign of enemy, clever bastards. The flare drifted north, and as it started to fade, the lead sections of 2 Platoon were moving into the bowl, down to our left. As it went dark, the lead section was smashed by numerous streams of orange and green, from all around the bowl. I aimed at the muzzle flash just right of my arc, and began firing bursts into it. My own muzzle flash blinded me, but I could still see where my target was firing from. Burst after burst went into it, but the fucker kept firing.

"Come down slightly!" Jamie screamed in my ear, correcting my fire. I did as he said, and began to get somewhere. I hammered my target with some heavy bursts, and it fell silent for the time being.

"Next target left!" screamed Jamie again. I switched to the next muzzle flash, putting heavy bursts into it. But then the original position burst into life again. I had to remain on the bunker I was committed to, and kept firing.

There was a heart-stopping clunk. Shit, shit, shit. "Stoppage!" I cried out, as I grabbed the carry handle and dragged myself and the gun into cover. Staying in the same position to clear a stoppage is something that would seriously upset lovers and mothers, since machine-gunners in those situations are pure bullet magnets. The reduced firepower was evident in our group, as the enemy were not only dealing with 2 Platoon down below, but were also smashing fuck out of the rocks our group was behind. Be quick, Archie boy, be real quick. Cock gun, belt off, check for the problem, solve the problem, clear the gun and put the belt back on, back in action, done.

   As I got the gun back into the fight, 2 Platoon was fighting for its life in the bowl. They were trying to clear out the bunkers around the base of the bowl anti-clockwise. Several guys rushed up just short of a bunker, only to be mowed down by another bunker opposite. As the orange and green splashed into and around them, the lead guy dropped like liquid, bayonet sticking in the ground, which kept him propped up in a kneeling position. A second guy tripped over him, and as he scrambled to his feet, was blown in half by rounds hitting the grenades in his pouches, showering him across the front of the position they were trying to assault. A third guy went for the target bunker, but the enemy gunner took his head off with a savage burst from his machinegun. 2 Platoon's fury intensified, as they gave this particular bunker everything they had, which in turn riddled the propped-up body with ricochets and grenade splinters. The bunker fell silent, and its occupants had better be dead, I don't think 2 Platoon were in the mood for a quiet chat.

   We continued to hammer the remaining muzzle flashes, and little by little, A Company started to make progress. Our group and 1 Platoon would smash fuck out of a position, with what was left of 2 Platoon creeping up and throwing grenades in. As each series of dull thuds were heard, we switched our attention to the next bunker, as 2 Platoon went into the last one, making sure them fucks were finished. Grim but effective.

What seemed like forever, we slowly dealt with the enemy in the bowl. The bowl gradually became just a mixed bag of random shots, and the odd thud of grenades in bunkers. What a night. One of the guys from 1 Platoon crawled over to our group and thanked us for our help. A Company was going to reorganise and start to push east, clearing the remainder of Longdon.

We crawled back to the top of the alley. The gun teams on the summit were still taking on targets further east, but not as intense as before the assault into the bowl. Jay rounded us up. "Good work guys, good shooting." We didn't feel too pleased about ourselves to be honest. 2 Platoon got chewed up pretty bad in the bowl, but the position was taken. It could have been a lot worse, I suppose. "Once A Company has sorted themselves out," Jay continued, "we will make our way to the RAP for a breather, we've earned it. Besides, we've got some messed-up guys that need taking down there."

He was right, we were in bad shape. And on the horizon, daylight was starting to make an appearance. A fog was also starting to take hold, which made the cold even more intense. As my adrenaline began to subside, I began to shiver big time, partially due to the cold, but also from what had taken place during the course of the night. Hopefully, daylight would bring some comfort, and we could sort ourselves out properly in the RAP.

CHAPTER 10: The Fallen

We left 1 Platoon on the edge of the bowl, and we slowly made our way back down the alley to 4 Platoon's rendezvous point. Upon our arrival, we noticed some of the less seriously wounded, helping the medics get the real messed-up guys sorted. Their platoon sergeant rallied up the guys, and asked us to help get his boys to the RAP, which was but a short distance away. One of his guys that needed help was a lad who took a load of grenade fragments to the face. He was sitting, his face covered in a field dressing. His jaw was exposed and splattered in his blood, and the field dressing had clearly been on a while, since blood was starting to seep through. I leant down and took him by the arm, which made him jump. "Hello mate," I said, "I'm Archie."

"Hello Archie," he replied, "have you got a cigarette please?"

Bloody typical. I didn't smoke, but I didn't want to disappoint him. "Hang on," I told him, "back in a tick." I approached one of the other 4 Platoon lads for a cigarette.

He accompanied me back to my patient, lit a cigarette, and put it between his lips. "There you go, Kev," the lad said. "Blind or not, get your own fags out in future, you tight bastard." Gallows humour never fails.

Kev appeared rather content, now he had a cigarette on the go, and must have sensed me stood there, as he put his hand out towards me. I grabbed him by the wrist and hauled him to his feet. I steadied him, and then I turned around, ensuring his hand had hold of my webbing yoke straps, since I would need my hands free to use the gun if need be.

Jay made sure we were all set to go, and slowly led us away. We began to skirt around to the right. As we cleared some craggy rocks on our right-hand side, I could make out a number of figures in the early morning mist, milling about 200 metres ahead on the right.

As we got closer, we could see people helping others into a rocky outcrop. As we drew near, it became apparent this was A Company, bringing their wounded into the RAP from the bowl. A lone figure stood out from the others in the open ground, and judging by his body language, he appeared to be running things.

Jay turned to us, and told us to sit tight, so he could find out where the RSM wanted us. So OB, the RSM, was the lone figure. OB was as old-school as they came. I bumped into him a few times, not always on the best of terms. He was firm but fair, and as he came over to us, the sight before him must have appeared rather pathetic. Stood before him were the shattered remains of 4 Platoon, plus a few from 5. He pointed to an area not too far from the A Company lads. "Get yourselves in there lads, get yourselves sorted, get a brew and some food in and keep warm." He wasn't a brash sergeant major on the drill square; he was gentle, kind, almost fatherly.

We made our way over to where he wanted us, and we set about getting the wounded comfortable. I carefully sat Kev down and helped him out of his fighting gear. I then opened his canvas roll on his belt kit, and helped him into his quilted suit, then his waterproofs, just to keep the wind off him. It quickly dawned on me that I had none of my warm kit with me. It was all in my barrel bag, where I'd left it during the initial contact. Dickhead. I took my webbing off and sat on it. The cold started to seep in, and I shivered like mad, really wanting my warm gear. I had been cold during the night, but during the fighting, you forgot about the cold, since there were more pressing issues at hand. Jamie moved over to me and plonked himself down. He opened his canvas roll, and gave me his waterproof jacket. "It's not exactly quilted, but it will keep the wind off."

I accepted it, and wasted no time getting it on, material rustling and Velcro tearing as I fought my way into it. I must get my barrel bag; it had all my warm kit in it, including my waterproofs. I felt like such an amateur. I should have known better. Jamie winked at me and gave me a cheeky grin. Bastard. I returned his kind gesture by getting the kettle on, rummaging through my pouches for hot chocolate, and whatever treats I had left from my rations. It wasn't long before we had the biggest mug of hot chocolate ever to be dished out, between us and the 4 Platoon guys. A couple of sips made you feel like a new man, everything felt good for a while. Once it was finished, someone else got a hot cup of something on the go. Even in battle, there was always time for a cuppa.

Our mood was subdued instantly, when we heard the thump of grenades and the cracking of gunfire, off to our right along the mountain. A Company was once again clearing out the enemy, which still occupied the eastern end of Longdon. Screams were the soundtrack of close combat and the use of bayonets. The screams went right through you. Please get it done quickly, guys, get it done.

Jamie nudged my arm and pointed off to the left. Out of the closing fog, scarecrows of men began to emerge, carrying their grim cargos of wounded men. 5 and 6 Platoon made their way into the RAP. The RSM went to meet them and pointed in our direction. They slowly made their way amongst us, putting the wounded down wherever there was room.

Davo stood up and signalled to us with a small hand gesture to move back to 5 Platoon, our secondment to 4 was at an end. We got settled back with our own platoon. It was comforting to be with more familiar faces. They did however look hollow shattered shells of men, which seemed fair enough, considering the night we'd just had. Did we look like that to them? They didn't say. Medics clucked around the guys that needed them, and out to the front of our location were Justin and Dale. Dale was armed with a notebook and pen; I could tell he was in deep consultation with the OC about Company business. It was hardly surprising. B Company had been badly mauled during the night, and not everyone was accounted for. By the look of things, all the wounded had been brought to the RAP, so that just left the dead, B Company dead. You didn't need to be an atomic scientist, to hazard a wild guess of what was to be asked of us next.

Dale and Justin walked over to address their battered and bloodied Company. Dale did the talking. "Guys, firstly myself and the OC would like to thank you tremendously for your efforts during the night, we secured the western end of the objective, but due to heavy resistance, we had to hand the task over to A Company." He paused to allow it to sink in. "Having checked the Company nominal roll, we have several unaccounted for. We must ask something more of you before we finish here. Not yet however. Get some rest and hot food. Once A Company has finished on task, we know what we have to do."

He turned to Justin, who by the look of things was trying his hardest to hold it together. Dale took him gently by the arm and led him in to the rocks, a little way from us. Justin's Company had taken a real battering, and he just needed some fatherly reassurance from his Company Sergeant Major, the most seasoned soldier in the Company, that his plan and decisions had been the right course of action. They settled down with what remained of Justin's group, which amongst the rocks was nothing more than a series of helmets and radio antennas bobbing around.

Gunfire and the thud of grenades continued further along the mountain, as A Company took care of business. I'm sure it wouldn't be long before they would start ferrying more of their guys back to the RAP. We couldn't make out who was doing the shooting and grenade lobbing; the enemy could be counterattacking, for all we knew. The only indication of who was doing the damage was that you could tell a trained soldier from his short controlled bursts of a machinegun, the wild erratic long bursts being those of an amateur. Not much else. There was plenty of shouting and screaming up on the feature, but you couldn't make out if it was English or Spanish. Before long, the fighting petered out to the odd burst of gunfire and thud of grenades.

Dale emerged from his perch amongst the rocks, and called for our attention. "Guys, let's do this. All platoons will back-track their route here. Carefully make your way up your original routes, checking bunkers and any dead you encounter, including enemy. Take caution however. Some sneaky bastards may have booby trapped the dead, theirs and ours. You are to keep out of sight of Tumbledown to the south, which is still occupied. Some of 'em may emerge from bunkers we missed in the advance, and surrender. So be on your game, understand?"

We nodded, and began to get our gear back on. Dale waved his arms. "Weapons and smocks only, belts and mags ready to use." Happy with that, I handed Jamie back his waterproof, confident I would find my barrel bag, and my precious warm kit. I had a belt of about fifty rounds on the gun, and I wrapped another two hundred around me, just in case we encountered trouble.

We began to move out, 4 Platoon leading, then us, with what was left of 6 behind. Company HQ stayed at the RAP for now. It wasn't long before 4 skirted up, and around to the left into the alleys, where they had faced the grim task of carving the enemy out of their stronghold. Despite the fog, the early morning light made identifying features and positions much easier. Most of the bunkers 4 had dealt with during the night were still smouldering from their destruction with grenades, both high-explosive and white phosphorous. We continued past the bunkers, and around the large rock slabs that divided the mountain, like a large toast rack. It wasn't long before we could see the ground we had cleared in the darkness. More smouldering bunkers marked our progress. On our left side, we passed close to a bunker that had a caved-in timber roof. My stomach turned over. It quickly dawned on me that it was the bunker I fell in. Jamie knelt down on the edge of it and inhaled. "Wow, something is cooking a treat in there." What was cooking would be the two guys I fell on. It could have been so different if they were ready for me, as I came crashing through their roof.

Davo called for our attention. "Guys, break down into pairs, and check all the positions you can find. Any dead you encounter, check them too, and remember to look out for booby traps. No funny stuff."

Everyone spread out, but Jamie and I stayed put. I turned my back to the bunker, trying to retrace my route to my barrel bag. There was a series of rock clusters between where we were, and the open ground where we had our start line. We made our way between the clusters and found evidence of the night's fighting; webbing, brass casings, medical kit. No bodies however. These may have been the first pieces of cover for the Company, when it all kicked off. Before we reached the open ground, we both stopped. I turned around and faced back up the mountain. In the morning light, it didn't look as steep as it had in the darkness. During the night, it had felt like we were fighting our way up a cliff face. I looked over to my right and saw another cluster of rocks, and we made our way to it. On one side of the rocks were some fresh empty cases, and some belt link from a machinegun. This must be it. A little way out from the rocks was a sorry-looking canvas bag, shredded beyond use. My barrel bag. I rummaged through it. Everything in it had been badly battered. The spare barrels were chipped beyond use. My quilted suit didn't look fit to go on a scarecrow. My waterproofs were half-shredded, and half-melted to the barrels. What bastards shot fuck out of my kit? I was too cold to be fussy at this point. My woollen jersey didn't look too bad, and I wasted no time getting it on. Straight away, having another layer on was pure bliss. I didn't care about its appearance. It would be under my smock, and therefore Dale wouldn't spot it, and chew me out for my trampish appearance. I took what remained of the barrel bag, and slung it over my back. It would have to do. We then began to slowly make

177

our way up the feature, and help the guys search for dead and wounded.

  As we picked our way through the rocks, we saw a few of the guys up ahead. They were stood over what could only be a bunker or something. As we pulled up next to them, a horror show laid at our feet. We had found Tony, and what appeared to be Kyle. I could feel the burning bile, as it tried to rise up into my mouth, but I managed to keep it down. Both had been riddled with bullet holes and grenade splinters. They were past bleeding out; their blood had soaked through their clothing, and the peat around them. The way they had met their deaths was clear to see. Tony was on his back with his smock and shirt open, with what appeared to be a horrific chest wound, and Kyle was slumped over his midriff, hands full of field dressings, clearly trying to save his platoon commander's life. Their bodies had clearly been caught in the crossfire of soldiers, fighting in the darkness. Tony's helmet had been smashed by a number of rounds, but yet his face remained intact. Kyle had not been so lucky. He had taken entry wounds, clean through the face, but the back of his helmet was missing, along with the contents of his head, giving the appearance of a scooped-out eggshell. We just stood there, taking in the scene.

Davo eventually broke our silence. "Get Kyle's poncho, and cover them over. Mark their position with one of their rifles." We looked at each other for a moment, none of us wanting to touch them. Davo rolled his eyes and knelt down behind Kyle. "For fuck's sake," he cursed under his breath, loud enough for us to hear. He undid Kyle's canvas roll on top of his webbing pouches, and began to unwrap his poncho. I took this as my cue to pick up one of their weapons, and point it muzzle down in the peat, deep enough for it to stand unaided. Jamie and Leighton helped Davo spread out the poncho, and draped it over the bodies. Davo held up his hand. "Wait. Ammo, water and rations, they don't need them anymore."

This was not what I had in mind, but he was right, we needed those precious commodities now. I knelt down behind Kyle and went through his pouches. I found six full magazines for his rifle, including the one I had removed from his weapon. Two water bottles were almost full, and there was a mixed bag of sweets, a brew kit and biscuits. We couldn't get to Tony's kit in his webbing, but Davo went through his smock, for his map and compass. Once done, we placed the poncho over them again, and weighed the corners down with whatever rocks or ballast was available to hand.

"Let's check the rest of the area," Davo ordered. "We can come back for these guys later." We made our way further up the feature, towards the top of the saddle, and it was then I saw what the enemy looked like, up close and somewhat dead. One particular bunker we discovered had a couple of drab olive tents, partially collapsed behind it. You couldn't see the tents until you were right on top of the position, since they had been concealed and protected by a series of large rocks. In front of the bunker entrance were two bodies in drab olive quilted jackets, drab olive denims, but no boots or socks. These guys were completely riddled with bullet holes. There were large dried blood patches underneath them, where they had bled out all over the peat. One of them had a radio handset clutched in one hand, and a rosary in the other. The other was lying on top of what looked like his personal weapon, but he had a magazine in his right hand. These guys must have been fighting, when our lads piled into the protected campsite. The tents behind them were a sorry sight. Both were riddled with bullet holes and grenade splinters. The right tent still held its unfortunate occupants, killed in the dark, whilst still in their sleeping bags. One of them had attempted to scramble out the back end of the tent, half out of his sleeping bag and half-dressed, his face caved in by heavy gunfire. The left tent appeared unoccupied, but blood was evident around its base. Maybe these guys had survived the assault, and had escaped the carnage. This position had been destroyed with extreme violence by our guys. Jamie went forward, and without ceremony prodded the bodies with the muzzle of his rifle. Dead for sure.

There was a clatter of metal to our left, and we could see a pale hand waving at us, from a small hole amongst the rocks and peat. Weapons at the ready, we formed a base line and faced the hand. There appeared the green dome of a helmet, then a pale face. Davo took a step forward, and pointed his weapon at the face. "Out now!" he growled. "Get the fuck out, or we will shoot."

Another hand appeared. The person shuffled his shoulders, revealing his torso. He then scrambled out quickly, so his feet were clear, and rolled on his back with his hands in the air. Our first prisoner. Davo stormed over to the hole, with us covering the guy on the floor, and began to demand that anyone else in the hole surrender. Nothing. He clicked his fingers at the guy on the floor to get his attention, who very quickly got the gist of what Davo was about to do. Davo had pulled a grenade from a pouch, and made it clear he was going to frag the hole. The prisoner then ranted something loudly in Spanish towards the hole, over and over. Movement and commotion could now be heard inside. Another pair of hands appeared, followed by a mop of black greasy hair. Davo put the grenade back in his pouch, and leaned in and grabbed the second person by the scruff of the neck, dragging him out. The second prisoner gagged and choked, as he was pulled alongside the first.

Davo returned to the hole. Were there anymore in there? One of the enemy soldiers waved his hands. No more, that was it. Davo quickly peeked into the hole, clear on what he wanted to happen next. "Archie, cover them. Zane, Jamie, search them now."

Leighton moved over to Davo, who was preparing a grenade for the follow-up. Davo pulled the pin, and in it went. A few seconds later, there was a loud thud, followed by smoke drifting from the hole. Jamie and Zane went to work searching our prisoners, who were both lying flat on their backs, arms outstretched. Zane and Jamie were a bit hesitant to start with, but soon got their groove, checking the prisoners over methodically. Watch, wallet with a few photos of family, a rosary, some cigarettes. Nothing that led us to believe they were of any importance, just two conscripts hoping not to get killed today. Well, their luck was in. Zane got to his feet. "Nothing, no maps or command kit, just soldiers."

We looked up the mountain, and saw the remainder of the platoon, having the same experience as us. Enemy soldiers began to appear, out of the slimmest of gaps in the rocks. They must have sat tight and silent through last night, praying they wouldn't be discovered. Since the largest group of prisoners was above us, we pulled our two to their feet, and moved them up to join their comrades. As we arrived, the group of prisoners was laying face down, side-by-side with their hands on their heads. We put our two on the left end of the line, and they copied the others.

"Gunners stay here and watch this lot," Davo called out. "The remainder of you keep searching." Being a gunner, I got babysitting duty, whilst the lads went further up the feature, searching for our dead, and with a bit of luck, maybe some wounded. I looked over to where the remainder of our platoon were gathered. They were stood around the bodies of the two guys that knocked out the problem bunker in the night. From what I could see, they carefully laid the sitting body down on its side, as if not to wake him. As for the guy in front, he was almost burnt to a cinder. Ponchos and blankets appeared, and two rifles were placed muzzle down in the ground, to mark the bodies as ours.

Out of some rocks to the right, what appeared to be 6 Platoon came into view, amongst them a handful of prisoners. The prisoners were placed onto our line. Not including 4 Platoon, B Company had a fair size bag of prisoners. If all these had put up a fight last night, some of us could have been under a blanket marked with a rifle. Two further figures appeared below us. As they drew near, we made out the profiles of Dale and Justin. As they pulled up, Dale let out a whistle. "Fucking hell boys, look at this lot."

One of the 6 Platoon lads piped up. "How is 4 getting on?"

"They've got a couple of prisoners who are wounded," Justin answered. "No one else, I don't think 4 were in the mood to be nice last night."

"Right guys," Dale cut in. "Let's not bite off more than we can chew, get these fuckers down to the RAP."

A high-pitched screech sounded. Shell fire began to smash, all over the top of the saddle. We scattered in amongst the rocks around us. The prisoners stayed where they were, squirming uncomfortably, wanting the shelling to finish. Heavy shell fire smashed the saddle and the backside of the feature, really making the ground beneath us shudder. Shells thudded and smashed into the open ground, just in front of our start line. It all lasted a few minutes, but seemed much longer. Once it had finished, we carefully emerged from our cover. The prisoners were crying and squirming nonstop.

"They have lost this position," announced Justin, proudly. "That's their defensive fire plan. Shell their own positions, and deny them to us."

"Beautiful," said an anonymous voice from amongst the 6 Platoon lads, "just what I always wanted." There was some nervous giggling amongst our boys. They began to pull the prisoners to their feet, and lead them off the feature, down and around to the RAP. I didn't want to lead, so I hung back, until the prisoners began to be shepherded down the mountain.

Davo hung back next to me, looking at me, like he wanted to say something. "We found Danny, and John and Brandon," he eventually murmured.

"Where?" He didn't answer, just flicking his eyes to the sitting body. "Shit, really?" I said. "Who....?" I couldn't get my words out straight.

"Danny was the one sitting," he explained. "John was the one that caught fire. Brandon and two enemies were in the bunker, it was real messy in there." He looked so sad. He began to well up. I was stunned for words; three platoon characters killed, dealing with one bunker, fuck. "We will come back for them," he undertook, "once we've dealt with these prisoners. Don't want to be overstretched, just in case they counterattack." He managed to compose himself, and it was then business as usual.

CHAPTER 11: Plunder

As Davo and I drew just short of the RAP, A Company were bringing in their prisoners, and OB called out for ours to join them. Our prisoners were dropped off with some of what I believed to be A Company lads, who were assigned to guard them. Some prisoners had carried in their dead, and had piled them up without ceremony, in front of where they were told to sit. It made for grim viewing. The dead appeared to be department store dummies, badly dressed. The uniforms hanging off them revealed the grim nature of their deaths. Bullet holes, grenade splinters, bayonet puncture wounds. Some were missing heads altogether, their jackets soaked black with their blood. What I found most bizarre was the fact that most of the dead had no boots on, or were in just a shirt and trousers. Were these guys caught half-dressed in their positions? Fighting and dying on what they slept in? The sight was not what I was expecting. I had this romantic image in my tiny mind, of dying with blazing guns to an awesome soundtrack, not getting my head blown off or bayoneted in the face, whilst struggling to get out of my sleeping bag.

We moved into a clump of rocks. I found my webbing, and dumped my poor excuse of a barrel bag next to it. Dale came over to me. "What the hell happened to that?" he enquired.

I came clean. "I took it off at my first piece of cover, sir, and it got fragged."

He shook his head and chuckled. "Well, Archie boy, just think. If you'd been wearing it, when it got the good news, we'd be covering you with a poncho." Shit, he had a point. "Is your warm kit shagged?" he pursued.

"Yes sir. And it's not getting any warmer." This wasn't far from the truth. The early morning fog had all but disappeared, revealing a brilliant but freezing cold sky.

"Well," he said, looking at the pile of enemy dead. Then he looked at me with a serious glare. "You won't have to go too far to shop for new stuff, will you?" I just looked at him, hoping he wasn't serious. "Let's be clear on this, Archie, they don't need it anymore, do they?" Holy shit. He walked off. I sat down, stunned.

Jamie came and sat with me, digging into his webbing for his brew kit. Without waiting for me to offer, he leaned over and pulled out my hot chocolate, and one of my water bottles. I started to shiver again. It was getting colder. Without the activity of the last hour or so, my body began to cool down again. Jamie rabbited away, and you know what? I wasn't listening to a word of it. I just looked at my hands, and then the pile of bodies, then back at my hands.

He jabbed me in the arm, which snapped me out of my own world. "Are you ignoring me?" he demanded.

"What?"

"I said, do you want me to cook you some scoff?" He rolled his eyes.

"Yeah, cheers." I dug into one of my webbing pouches, and threw him a bag of instant porridge.

"What did Dale say?" he asked. "Did he give you a bollocking for the barrel bag?" I looked at my sorry-looking barrel bag, and it dawned on me that Dale wasn't really that interested in it.

"No, he asked if my warm kit was still in good shape. If not, where to get some."

"Where to get some? The quartermaster is at Estancia." He looked at the pile of bodies, and then back at me. His smile quickly disappeared, becoming a look of horror. He didn't say anything else. He looked down and took great interest in our porridge, in a mess tin on the burner. We sat in silence whilst the water came to the boil, neither of us wanting to talk about what Dale had implied. He then raised his head, as a high-pitched thunder roared over the mountain, and thumped into the open ground to the north of us. Shells smashed into the summit, and further along the feature amongst A Company's positions. For every shell that smashed into the mountain, two would thud on the open ground. It became clear that the RSM had sited the RAP well. The shelling would not hit us directly, but it didn't make you any more comfortable to be shelled in the first place. The prisoners all huddled in together, hands on their ears, since the noise and concussion was immense. Being shelled is one thing, being shelled by your own side is a real shit day at the office. We turned over onto our bellies. Our breakfast was almost ready to be eaten. Every now and again, we'd have to hold the mess tin in place, so the vibration of the explosions wouldn't ruin our efforts.

The shelling ended as quickly as it started. Once the echo of the explosions faded away, we heard commotion above us, and calls for medics. Someone was hurt, didn't know which side. At this time, we were all in the same boat.

Casualties from the shelling began to arrive at the RAP. It was starting to get rather crowded, and Dale came to a decision. "B Company, listen up. If you are not wounded, move back up onto the summit, so room can be made down here for those that need it. Locate decent cover, so you've got somewhere to go when they shell us again, which they probably will. Get your gear, and don't go east of the bowl. Move now."

We got to our feet. Jamie grabbed my arm. "Let's go do it, so we don't have to come back down here again."

We made our way over to the pile of enemy dead. None of them looked pretty; the cause of their demise was clear to see. Jamie began to strip off his gear as three prisoners arrived, dragging one of their dead by the ankles. Two had hold of the ankles, dragging the body as if they didn't have a care in the world. I think I can safely say our dead were not being dragged to the RAP in that manner. The body was naked from the waist up, and without a head. The third prisoner was carrying the missing body part, cradling it in his arms, his face void of any emotion. They didn't try to put the body on the pile. They just left it alongside, the head placed on top of the body. Grim.

The three prisoners made their way over to where their comrades were sat. Jamie began to circle the pile, checking out what was on special offer. I was after a duvet jacket, with as minimal evidence of its previous owner as possible. When new, the jackets would have looked the business. I took my fighting gear off, and began to look more into what the dead were wearing. Pickings were slim; the jackets I was interested in were in real bad shape. I couldn't wear a jacket soaked in blood, brain and snot of its former owner. Not only was it a serious moral issue, but clearly wasn't hygienic.

Jamie let out a whistle. "What about this one?" I moved around the pile, and at his feet was a potential candidate. The body was free of blood, so it appeared, fully dressed and in fairly good shape. One could only imagine what had killed him, with such minimal damage. His arms were outstretched, giving the impression he had been frozen solid, trying to strangle someone. Strange. We knelt, taking hold of his jacket and trouser legs, turning him on his side to inspect the back. No damage there either. I was puzzled.

"What the fuck happened to him?" I said out loud.

"Blast," came a voice on the other side of the pile, "probably naval gunfire."

We both scrambled to our feet, only to see Dale. "OB said to be quick about it and fuck off," he warned, "before you get lynched by that lot." We swung around. The prisoners were getting rather irate about our interest in their dead comrades. The lads guarding them started to get heavy handed, making them sit down and be quiet.

"We have a jacket," piped up Jamie. "It's not going to be easy getting it off without some reshaping, if you get my drift."

"Get on with it," Dale demanded through gritted teeth. Without hesitation, Jamie pushed me to one side, and stamped on the right arm of the body, resulting in an almighty crack. I looked away as my stomach turned over, spraying the ground beneath me with porridge and hot chocolate, that all too familiar burning sensation in full force, in my throat and mouth. Why did you do that, Jamie? I heard another crack, as he continued with his method of straightening a dead man's arms.

"Help me then, for fuck sake," he barked, as he pulled the body onto its front. "It's your bloody jacket."

I helped Jamie get the body turned over. He stood up, both hands clutching the jacket, his right boot firmly between the shoulder blades of its current owner. I felt rather faint. A few seconds later, the jacket was free. He slung it at me, as he jogged back to his kit. I didn't examine the goods straightaway. I followed him, getting kitted up in quick time, and walking briskly up to where Davo and the other lads had gathered at the entrance to the summit bowl.

CHAPTER 12: The Artillery Duel

As I looked around the summit bowl with Jamie, it was clear to see how brutal the fighting had been. We had been positioned high during the earlier battle, firing down and across, in support of the lads clearing the bunkers. But hidden further down in the bowl was a whole different story. There were bodies everywhere, theirs and ours. Even now, A Company was clearing out a few stubborn defenders to the east of the bowl, and had yet to come back to deal with their own dead. I hoped we didn't get spammed with clearing A Company casualties, since we still had to recover our own.

The first bunker I encountered had collapsed; its occupants were crushed under the weight of a huge slab of rock that had been its roof. An Argentine soldier was half hanging out of the position, right arm outside. He was slumped over, his head visible, his jaw crushed with dried blood, snot congealed all over the rock. In front of the bunker on the grass was the body of one of ours, face down, fully kitted up, and riddled with bullets and grenade splinters. I didn't know the guy, but he was a member of the Battalion nonetheless.

We started to climb back up the bowl, towards where we were during the night, giving fire-support. Over to our left

194

was a smouldering bunker which cost the lives of three men that had tried to storm it. One was still propped up by his rifle, his body smashed beyond recognition, having been caught in a furious crossfire. Lying next to him was the headless remains of his mate, who had clearly got a face full of machinegun fire. Across the opening of the bunker was the lower half of the third man, whose grenades must have been hit. Dried blood and internal organs were scattered over the rocks to the left of the bunker entrance. One could only imagine what was left of the occupants of the position, when the rather pissed off lads of A Company came to silence it for good.

Jamie and I found a relatively flat piece of ground, just below the upper rim of the bowl. Not too sure how much cover it would give us from shelling, but I didn't want to get into the bunkers, not knowing what state they were in inside. I took my gear off and sat on my webbing. With my back to some rocks, I had one hell of a view of the whole bowl, and the carnage that had taken place there in the dark. It wasn't long before the cold began to creep in again, and I examined my newly acquired duvet jacket. Jamie had chosen well. It was in good condition, but reeked of body odour. Its former owner must have put it on in Argentina, not taking it off since, as it smelt vile. But the cold air kept me from being too proud to wear it. It did fit rather nicely, and with the zip done up all the way to my chin, it certainly kept the cold out, and the foul odour inside. Beggars can't be choosers.

  As I leaned forward to adjust my seating position, I felt something digging into my right side. Undoing the zip and getting a fresh face full of dried sweat, I discovered an inside pocket. I put my hand in, and felt what had the texture of paper and plastic. I pulled the items out, to discover they were letters and a couple of laminated photos. The letters were in Spanish, so I therefore didn't have a clue what they said. They had a very mild scent of perfume, probably letters from a girlfriend. One photo was of a rather attractive young girl, probably the author of the letters. The other was what I could only guess to be his family, prior to his departure on the crusade to reassert Argentine pride. This young soldier was stood at the centre of the shot. His family flanked him, all looking very proud of their son or brother, doing his duty for his country. If only they knew he was now on a pile of badly smashed corpses, after having his life ripped from him by the blast of artillery. Looted of his clothing by enemy soldiers, one of whom now enjoyed the warmth his jacket provided, and was looking through his personal effects. If the roles were reversed, it would shatter my mum and dad.

A small group of prisoners came into the bowl, escorted by a couple of our guys. They made their way over to the first bodies in their way. The bodies were a mixture of theirs and ours, and judging by the way they were laid out, it had been gruesome hand-to-hand fighting, a real fight to the death. They were probably cut down in a frenzied fire fight, as A Company attempted to rush the positions in the darkness. I watched with interest as the prisoners carefully moved our dead to one side, probably fearing swift justice from their guards, should they be disrespectful. But the prisoners then grabbed the ankles of their own dead, and without ceremony began dragging them off towards the RAP, truly bizarre. Was this the way they dealt with their dead as a matter of course, or were they just a large group of strangers told to defend this mountain?

I looked again at the letters and photos in my hands; I didn't want to keep them as trophies. I got to my feet, leaving my kit with Jamie, who in typical fashion had a brew on the go. I jogged down a slope and caught the attention of the guys guarding the prisoners in the bowl. I walked up to the nearest prisoner, pulled his jacket open, and stuffed the letters and photos in his pocket. I gave him a friendly jab in his shoulder, and in return he gave me a slight grin and a nod. I turned on my heels and made my way back up to Jamie, hoping the soldier would look at the effects later, and understand what I wanted him to do. The effects shouldn't end up in a mass grave. Get them home. I sat back down on my perch, and Jamie passed the brew to me, coffee. "Out of chocolate, mate," he grinned, "coffee it is."

I wasn't bothered; I cupped it in my hands, enjoying the warmth, sipping it slowly. Below us, Davo and some of the guys were inspecting bunkers, even venturing into them. It became apparent what they discovered, when whoever went in poked their head back out to vomit, which the remainder found rather entertaining. It quickly began to dawn on me how tired I was. The warmth of the coffee and my new jacket made me drowsy; the adrenaline-fuelled night had drained from me as I began to relax. A rather bizarre sensation, considering the environment we were in right now, hardly serene. Freezing cold, death everywhere you looked. Smouldering bunkers that reeked of human shit, the smell of cordite from fired ammunition, one hell of a day at the office.

Four more of our men appeared in the bowl. They appeared to be A Company lads. Each had some kind of white sleeping bag tucked under their arms. What on Earth were the bags? They stood over their dead, and between them began to unfold the white objects. The penny dropped, as soon as they laid the bags alongside their dead comrades. The bags were body bags. They laid one flat, and between them began carefully lifting a body, sliding the bag underneath. Once they lowered the body, they folded the body bag flap over and zipped it up, done. They each grabbed a corner, and made their way down and out of the bowl, probably towards the RAP.

The same four lads appeared in the bowl a short while later, to repeat the process for another one of their dead. The pattern continued for some time. The last body to be dealt with was the propped-up body, which followed the grim remains of his two mates, who had tried to help him knock their target bunker out.

I had been expecting Dale to appear, and round us up for the same task with our own dead. Buy maybe that task was already in hand, given the manpower he had around him. I just hoped he didn't come looking for extra muscle. I don't think I could have faced the task of shovelling what was left of Brandon out of that bunker, which killed John and Danny also. I recalled it reeking of shit, when we passed it in the night. Call me callous if you like, but I was not going to volunteer for the task.

Jamie had watched the whole scene below us with a dead pan expression. Everything we had been exposed to during the last twelve hours or so, he took without so much of a whimper. The comedian within him seemed to have gone. He hadn't been shy with getting to grips with the bodies, when finding me some warm kit, leaving me to puke all over the shop. I was getting a bit worried about Jamie, he wasn't himself anymore. He appeared emotionless to everything we'd done so far, not happy-go-lucky, just business. But what did I know? Maybe it was the best way to deal with things, right now. I just hoped he would snap out of it, when it was all over. He peered over to me, about to speak. But he paused, his eyes narrowing to a glare. "What the fuck is that, on the front of your helmet?"

I peeled the helmet off my head, and inspected the front. It was smeared in what could only be described as a light-pink mush, with dark hair stuck in amongst the black tape and camo. It smelt vile. I could only guess it was the remains of the soldier's face that I had head-butted repeatedly in the bunker I fell in. My stomach turned over, but I had nothing to bring up, so all I had to deal with was the bile burning my throat, which I managed to keep down. I promptly grabbed the helmet with both hands, and rubbed the front of it on the peat and grass next to me.

"What happened when we got split last night?" he pressed.

I kept my eyes focused on the helmet. "I fell into a bunker; there were two of them in their sleeping bags."

I glanced up. Jamie had a wicked grin on his face. "Totally awesome, what did you do?"

Jamie, you bastard. "I shot the first one, but the other was in my face, before I knew it. I head-butted him again and again until he stopped moving. That's it."

"Cool," said Jamie, clearly impressed.

"Dale dragged me out the trench," I continued, "and finished them off with a white phos."

He chuckled. "That's fucking hardcore, mate, good for you."

Really? I thought.

Our conversation was cut short, by a commotion above and behind us. We stood up, and turned to see what was causing the noise. Just behind the rocks were a group of Argentine soldiers, along with a couple of ours. The group was gathered in a huddle, looking at the ground. Jamie and I scrambled up to a better vantage point. At the feet of the group was what appeared to be a wounded Argentine soldier, being tended by one of our medics.

We clambered up to assist, and it quickly dawned on me exactly where we were. We were at the top of the alley that we fought our way up last night. We must have missed the Argentine guy in the darkness, as we scrambled forward to support A Company in the bowl. Evidence of our presence here last night was clear to see, brass cases and spent link all over the place.

I took in the surroundings. Off to the east in the far distance was what I could only guess to be Port Stanley, our ultimate prize. Not the sprawling metropolis I had in my head, but the island's capital, all the same. I panned right, and the full imposing feature of Mount Tumbledown loomed over us, across a wide valley. I glanced back at the group. They had got their casualty ready to travel.

"Get off the fucking top, now!" I looked down to see Dale staring straight up at us, with others in attendance, empty body bags at their feet. As I quickly mustered the words in my tiny brain to justify our bold action, the roar of shells smashing into the cliffs above the alleys rendered me deaf, in a high-pitched whine of ringing eardrums. As I dropped to the deck, I could just make out the muffled screams of casualties, and people shouting 'incoming'. The Argentine casualty on the ground flinched wildly, as shell splinters smashed into him, and the ground around him. A near-miss rocked us, but the concussion of the shell burst his head like a tomato.

More shells began smashing into the rocks above us, and thudding into the peat on the exposed summit. Our medic was crawling towards me, his face all bloody, his right leg a mangled mess. Off to the right, one of the Argentine soldiers broke cover, and dashed over to him. Just as he reached the medic, another shell burst in the open ground, just off to the right. Without ceremony, the Argentine grabbed our medic, and dragged him into cover, but the Argentine breaking cover in the first place had been madness.

The shelling ended as suddenly as it began. I raised my head, and peered over to where I last saw Jamie. He looked back at me with thumbs up, thank heavens. The gorse and peat on the summit had caught fire and was smouldering badly. As my hearing returned, I could make out someone calling my name behind me. I turned around. It was Dale. "Let me know what you need, and we will get it up to you."

My head was still swimming, as I gave myself a moment to gather my thoughts together. I got myself into a kneeling position, not confident about admiring the view anymore. The prisoners and their guards emerged from whatever cover they had found during the shelling. Now they had one of ours to deal with, the medic. To their credit, they got him ready to move in quick time, under the direction of the Argentine, who had madly dashed out and saved him. The Argentine was jabbering away in Spanish, physically gripping his comrades, who were just sobbing wrecks of men. They lifted our medic, and began a slow and treacherous decent, en route to the RAP. Jamie and I moved forward, assisting with taking the weight of the medic, as we crossed the more technical parts of the climb. Once down onto better ground, Dale took over the casualty evacuation or CASEVAC, which left Jamie and I to return to our gear.

As we sat down, Dale called out to us. "Artillery duel," he said, looking toward Port Stanley, "theirs against ours."

"Oh," I said. That told me.

"Stay off the fucking top," he warned again, "do you hear me?"

We nodded. He moved off, following the group carrying the wounded medic. As he drew level with the rear Argentine, he lurched out and grabbed him. The prisoner stumbled and fell to his knees, and then slumped onto his back. We just sat there, not really sure what was taking place. Dale stood wide-legged over him, and then looked straight at us, unleashing his rarely seen fury. "Don't just fucking sit there, get here now!"

We legged it down towards the Company Sergeant Major in a flash, struggling to shoulder our weapons as we ran. As we pulled up, he was tearing at the prisoner's clothing. I recognized the guy straight away. It was the prisoner who saved our medic. "Quick," urged Dale, "look for wounds, anything."

We scrambled to get the prisoner's jacket open, his shirt open. No sign of blood or wound. Dale pulled out his clasp knife from his smock and cut the man's belt, frantically pulling down his trousers. There was blood. He cut free the man's soiled underwear. The man's groin was a mass of smeared blood and shit. Dale used the guy's underwear to wipe the vile grime away as best he could, in an attempt to find the wound. Nothing. "Roll him over," he barked at us.

We flipped the guy over, more blood and shit smeared all over his buttocks. Still couldn't find the wound. Dale then grabbed the man's trousers by the crotch, which was dark with blood, and yanked them down to the point where they couldn't get over his boots. "Part his legs," barked Dale again, "now!"

Jamie and I scrambled to get this guy's legs open, our hands slippery with blood. We revealed his penis and testicles. Just to the right of his testicles we found a puncture wound, half an inch wide and about two inches long. Blood pumped out in a rhythm which could only mean one thing, the femoral artery. Dale pulled a field dressing from his smock pocket, and ripped off the packaging.

"Sir," Jamie piped up, "we are going to need more than one."

"Fuck the wound," growled Dale. "Tourniquet, help me make it tight." The Argentine guy was groaning, delirious with both pain and blood loss. We flipped him onto his back, and promptly lifted his legs, so Dale could wrap the dressing above the wound, in towards the groin. Once in the right place, Dale pulled it fucking tight to stop the bleeding. The blood only seeped out slightly from the wound, so it must have been tight.

He used one of his blood-smeared fingers to write the letter 'T' on the man's forehead. Dale glanced at his watch, and then wrote the time just below the letter. Further down the CASEVAC chain, The 'T' would indicate to medics and surgeons that a tourniquet was fitted, and the time would let them know when it happened. Simple yet effective.

Jamie fished a dressing from his smock, and then took care to surround the wound, so it wouldn't get filled with mud and shit, during the journey to the RAP. Others arrived, and quickly got the guy into a poncho and dragged him away, leaving us and Dale sat on our own, amid blood-soaked peat and packaging. Dale pulled off his helmet, and wiped his brow with the back of a blood-smeared hand. "I think he will lose the leg."

"That was the guy that saved our medic," I observed.

Dale didn't answer. He wiped his hands on the grass around him, and looked up at the sky. I could see his eyes were now glazed with both emotion and exhaustion. Before he let his guard down altogether, he put his helmet back on, and got to his feet, straightening himself up. Back to business. "Grab your gear and get back to the RAP, the OC will brief the Company on the next phase of operations."

We nodded. He turned and walked away. Next phase, really? I wasn't sure if I had enough left in me to do much more at this stage. We hadn't slept since yesterday morning. Any food I took in would only be sprayed all over the bloody mountain, at every turn in this fucking fight.

We clambered to our feet, and slowly made our way back up to our kit. The short but steep climb really took it out of me, all my energy drained from the adrenaline of the last hour or so. As I reached for my webbing, I noticed my hands, covered in another man's blood, along with shit and peat. I fished out a water bottle and went to town, getting as much of the foul coating off as possible. Once satisfied, I looked for something to dry my hands on. My clothing was filthy, so I had to just let them dry naturally. I pulled out my leather gloves from my smock and slipped them on. I felt more confident handling food and drink with my gloves on, than I would with my bare hands. Jamie and I struggled into our kit. We trudged down towards the RAP, leaving the various work parties in the bowl, dealing with the dead.

The RAP was even busier than before, a real hive of activity. Fuck knows how, but a small helicopter was parked there, along with two over-snow vehicles favoured by the commandos. Small work parties were carrying stretchers over to the helicopter, which was nothing more than a plastic bubble, with two cocoon-like boxes on the running skids. Two stretcher casualties were hustled into the boxes. Once they were secured, the rotors began to turn. In next to no time, the little helicopter rose up slightly, and banked away to the north, hugging the ground we had followed as we approached the mountain, the night before. I took it the more seriously wounded got helicopter rides out, since what I could make out as walking wounded were getting bundled into the snow vehicles.

Over to our left amongst the rocks, was a large group of prisoners that had survived the night, and had surrendered when the time was right. They looked filthy, exhausted, and bloody young. They all had their hoods up and hands in their pockets, shivering uncontrollably. To be honest, we were faring no better. It was the training we had that got us through, I think.

Off to the right was the grim view of their dead. The pile was bigger, still exposed to the elements; many had their eyes open, staring straight back at us and their surviving comrades. Some of the dead were half-naked, does anyone ever get used to such sights? It again reminded me of pictures of Auschwitz, and other places like it. Whatever the generation, whatever the war, close combat is savage and grim, plain and simple.

Further along, we came across more wounded, theirs and ours. They were all mixed together with medics, again both theirs and ours, beavering away to get everyone patched up, and as comfortable as possible. Most of the wounded were sat in amongst the rocks, trying to keep warm wrapped in blankets, and sleeping bags that looked like they had seen better days. Some of the wounded looked in a real bad way, others just sat there passing the time of day, with a cigarette hanging from their lips. The more seriously wounded were on stretchers, heavily wrapped in blankets, with a comrade or medic holding up a saline drip for them.

The law of the land was no matter what side you fought for, if you were a serious case, you were seen first. Some humanity had to surface in this God-awful place. There was one of our guys, possibly the Medical Officer, dishing out instructions to the medics, either in English or terrible Spanish. He had a notebook in his gloved paws, placing casualties in priority order, for the ride out of there. Despite the grim setting, it all looked rather organised.

We continued on a short distance, and found some familiar faces in amongst the rocks; B Company, or what was left of it. The numbers were fewer than earlier in the day. Maybe the shelling was the cause of it; I didn't have the bottle to ask anyone. Archie, just find a spot and shut up! Jamie and I found a patch to settle in, took off our gear and sat on it. My newly acquired duvet jacket turned a few heads, not sure if it was the novelty factor or the smell; it was still ripe with its former owner's fragrance.

Davo stood up a short distance away and waved me over. I got to my feet. He led me a short distance from the lads. "Archie, get that jacket under your smock, the prisoners are not happy with the fact we've been taking boots and shit off their dead. Any press sniffing around in Stanley will have a field day with this shit, get it sorted."

"Sure thing, Davo, sorry."

"Don't sweat it, mate, we've all got jackets and boots. Their gear is far better than ours, just don't display the fucker, alright?"

"Sure thing, thanks for the heads-up." I was correcting my state of dress, when he nudged my arm, and pointed over to OB and Dale. At their feet was a long line of filled body bags, which judging by their consulting of notebooks, meant they were B Company dead.

Further along was another line of body bags, with another character stood over them, notebook at the ready. He must have been A Company's Sergeant Major. He looked too junior to be one. I didn't know his name, but you tended to just socialise with your own Company, most of the time.

The names of those that had been killed were clear to see in bold black marker pen, written on the sides of all the bags. Among them were Tony, Danny, John, Brandon and Kyle. That was just from our platoon, the remainder were made up from 4 and 6 platoons. I counted 23 bags in total, a heavy price for such a prize; this bloody mountain. Not as heavy a price as the Argentines had paid; at a guess their pile of dead was about 40 odd. The cost in wounded was also pretty outrageous on both sides. I couldn't even guess what the number of wounded was, since some had already been evacuated. I observed the work parties helping the walking wounded over to the snow vehicles, their war over, on their way to the rear for treatment. How far rear; Estancia, Teal, San Carlos? The main thing was they were getting the hell out of there.

The RAP was slowly emptying of wounded, as the helicopter and snow vehicles ferried them out of there. All around where we were sat, you could smell various aromas; human shit, the coppery tang of blood, hexamine tablets, various hot foods, burnt peat, and cordite from spent ammunition. It was a real feast for the nasal senses.

Dale came over to me. Jamie threw me some sterile wipes, and what looked like toothpicks. "Got those from the Medical Officer," advised Dale, "for your hands."

"Thanks sir," I said, "nice one." He went about his business. Jamie and I went to town on our hands, swabbing them down, and scraping all the crud from under our fingernails. At one point, it looked like we wouldn't have enough wipes, but we made good progress with our ablutions. With our hands all clean, it then dawned on me that the insides of my gloves were now a bio-hazard in the making. I stuffed the gloves in my smock. Only when my fingers were on the verge of frostbite, would they go back on. I then tucked into my food, confident my hands were good enough, as I was ravenous. The beef stew and hard tack biscuits didn't touch the sides.

Once fed, we sat on our kit, watching the world go by. Another salvo of shells screamed in, smashing all over the summit, and thumping into the open ground near our start line. When it all calmed down, it was clear everyone was OK, because no fresh wounded or dead came into the RAP.

I glanced at my watch. It was mid-afternoon and I was shattered. I rested my head on my forearms in an attempt to doze, but the cold was seeping through my clothing again, and the odd shell crashing into the summit made sleep impossible. I lifted my heavy head, and movement off to my right caught my eye. OB was dishing out more body bags to the prisoners, who reluctantly made their way over to their pile of dead comrades, to conduct a most God-awful chore. I rested my head back on my forearms, since I didn't want to watch the grim action, and lose my food all over again.

Just off to my right, both Justin and Dale stood up, and let off an almighty stretch. Dale then rallied the remains of his battered Company. "Gather round, guys, leave your gear and shit where it is."

We all clambered to our feet, groaning, and shuffled over to where the OC was stood. He politely asked for platoon commanders and platoon sergeants to be at the front, but all that amounted to was just a few corporals and Davo. What a night it had been. Justin looked rather shocked at the sight of his rather depleted chain of command. He quickly composed himself. "Gentlemen, what was assessed as just short of company strength defending the mountain, in fact transpired to be two companies plus engineer elements." He paused to let it sink in. No wonder we had to fight for every rock on this fucking mountain. "Information gathered from key prisoners indicates that the enemy were tasked with merely delaying us, so reinforcements from Port Stanley and Tumbledown could then hit us from the right side. This however never took place, which I'm sure we are all pleased about." No shit. "Just shy of company strength managed to disengage from us, and withdraw to their reserve positions on Wireless Ridge. Brigade is more than aware of how hard our fight was last night, and has now tasked our Second Battalion with clearing Wireless Ridge tonight." I bet Second Battalion loved receiving that news. "Second Battalion are currently in a concentration area," continued Justin, "where we crossed the river. At last light, they will begin their approach to their start line, northeast of here. They will have a huge amount of fire-support for this tonight, along with the Scots Guards going for Tumbledown, so stay this side of Longdon until further notice."

"Where do we fit into all this, sir?" Davo asked.

"As a Company, not at all. Fire Support Company is on this one. Once Wireless Ridge is secured, our C Company will sweep through and clear Moody Brook Barracks, and then advance to contact, to the racecourse just outside Stanley, and take care of that bloody artillery line." A lone shell ironically smashed into the summit, making us all flinch and giggle nervously. "Brigade is looking at the real possibility of street fighting, with us and Second Battalion securing the break-in point, and the commandos clearing the town, Scots Guards in reserve. The town is mostly made of wood, so it wouldn't take long before tracer and phos grenades burn the whole fucker to the ground." There was more nervous tittering. "Guys, C Company will be moving into the RAP at last light. We are to vacate here and push up into the alleys, in order to make room. For those that have the idea of moving into A Company's area for a ringside seat, I would advise against it. With this shelling, decent cover is slim picking for them, let alone for us as well." Fair point. "Another long night tonight, boys, and by first light tomorrow, the plan is for our forces to have the high ground overlooking Port Stanley, and then we can plan the break into the town itself. Any questions?"

There were none. Dale took over proceedings. "Right then, get your shit sorted. Section commanders; get your guys up into the alleys as soon as possible. Cover in there is pretty good. Use the bunkers if you have to. Dismissed."

We made our way back to our kit. Another long night lay ahead of us. If we were not involved with tonight's attacks, could we go to sleep? I was absolutely shattered. I'm sure the whole Company was chin-strapped. Davo was still in conversation with Dale about something, so we just sat on our webbing. It was getting colder again, my bare hands starting to feel the bite. My minging gloves were last resort. I crossed my arms and wedged my hands under my armpits. It took the edge off, but not much.

Davo walked over. "Let's go, follow me." What remained of our section clambered to its feet, and we struggled back into our fighting gear. It was either getting heavier, or we were just running out of steam. We shuffled along behind Davo, and fell into single file. We skirted left around the base of the alleys, and slowly began to climb up into them. It wasn't long, before we came across the first bunkers 4 Platoon had knocked out, but Davo walked right on past, and led us straight up the alley. He turned, just short of the top. "This'll do, the cover here isn't bad. If a shell gets in here, then that's just real shit luck."

I was too tired to complain, the short sharp climb had almost killed me. The duvet jacket under my smock had me hotter than hell, but it wouldn't be long before the sweat would dry, and I would be a shivering wreck once again. Removing our gear, some of the lads began to explore where we had fought in the darkness. Some even attempted to scale the rock walls, and check out the enemy positions. I moved up to the top of the alley, where Davo and Jamie were perched. They were just eye level with the lip at the top, with the eastern end of Longdon in view, and Wireless Ridge and Port Stanley further beyond. Flanked left and right by sheer slabs of rock, we were in reasonable cover. Should we take a shell in here, then it would simply be bad fucking luck, plain and simple.

Davo got his brew kit out, and got the kettle on the go. Jamie salvaged some chocolate and biscuits from his smock, and offered them around. I got comfortable squatting on my webbing, with my back against the rock wall. It became very noticeable that the whole fucking mountain reeked of human shit. Did the Argentinians just drop their arse, anywhere they liked? Basic sanitation did not appear to be on their list of priorities, when occupying this position. Ideally you should have a latrine of sorts dug, and everyone uses that, but there were turds everywhere. We could have just got plenty of kip at Estancia, and wait for the Argentinians to die of plague, certainly the better option, considering what we had experienced last night and this morning.

I was starting to smell a bit funky with the duvet jacket on. I stripped off my smock, and then unzipped the jacket. The aroma of sweat and body odour hit me full force, which made me retch, causing Jamie and Davo to chuckle. "You might want to air that bad boy, mate," Davo mused.

"Yeah, good idea," I agreed. I pulled the jacket off, pulling through the sleeves, so it ended up inside out, the cold mountain air whipping around my exposed torso, which was still wrapped in my shirt and woollen jersey. I laid the jacket out to air, and with a bit of luck, the aroma of its former owner would vanish. The cold seeped into my core straightaway, making me shiver again. It was refreshing for a short period, but the smock soon went back on, just to take the bite off. By the time I'd finished pratting around, the brew was ready, and I was handed the metal mug. It felt great with my hands wrapped around it, and upon first sip, it was a gift from the gods, hot chocolate.

The hot chocolate went around us for what seemed forever, but all too soon it was finished, and Davo had packed his gear away. There wasn't much else to do; we couldn't go on the top, and risk getting caught in the open again. Off to the west of us, we heard a distant booming sound, followed by a faint streaking noise over the top of us, which faded away in the direction of Port Stanley. Then there would be the repeat again, but from the direction of Port Stanley streaking west.

The artillery duel continued for some time, both sides trying to knock each other out. Every now and again, a shell would thump into Longdon, amongst A Company's positions. The Argies were reminding us that they hadn't forgotten we were here. On the horizon, the light began to fade, the cold intensifying, and our breath was now very prominent in the air around us. By this stage, I couldn't handle the cold anymore. The duvet jacket was back on; it smelt a little bit better.

CHAPTER 13: Wireless Ridge and Mount Tumbledown

It was almost dark. The artillery duel had petered out. Maybe both sides were now just limbering up for another night of carnage. It started to snow. Light flakes of white slowly drifted across the mountain, settling on the rocks where it fell. The cold was even more intense now, the gloves becoming a more alluring prospect with each passing moment. We had passed the point where we could start cooking, bearing in mind we had line of sight with whoever was occupying Wireless Ridge. The faint glow of a hexi burner could be enough for their artillery observer on Wireless or Tumbledown to make a fine adjustment for the next salvo to come screaming in here, so it wasn't worth the risk.

In the far distance, Port Stanley was lit up, for all to see. Street lights, lights on in houses, headlights moving up and down the street, without a care in the world. Truly bizarre. Right on their doorstep, troops were carving and blasting each other to bits in the mountains above them, completely bonkers. There was movement at the bottom of an alley; I could make out the shapes of a large group of soldiers. I tapped Davo on the shoulder and pointed towards them.

"C Company," he stated. I was glad he paid attention during the briefings. I went back to looking at Port Stanley.

The ultimate prize was within our grasp; hot running water, baths and showers, beds, clean sheets, solid shelter from the weather. How many teenagers do you know, who would give these basic needs the time of day? To me at this point, they were priceless.

Davo stood up and began stamping his feet, getting the blood flowing again. If it was good enough for him, it was good enough for me and Jamie. My knees creaked, and my numb arse began to come back to life. Davo rummaged through his gear and pulled out his night scope. He put it to his eye and scanned away to the north. "Second Battalion are moving into position, by the looks of it."

He handed the scope to me. I was rather conscious of how exposed we were, but darkness was our friend, for the time being. I put the scope to my eye. It gave you a very bright, light-green image in the darkness, revealing our Second Battalion, moving very slowly in their heavily loaded columns toward their start lines. I didn't envy them. This was their second battle. By the sound of things, Goose Green had really set the tone for this land campaign. I felt a pang of guilt, since Wireless Ridge was meant to be one of our objectives. The enemy strength, and with it their resistance on Longdon, really put us in the hurt locker, resulting in one hell of a body count on both sides.

The distant thunder of our guns began. Projectiles streaked overhead, en route to their mark. The shells began to burst above Wireless Ridge, bathing the whole feature in brilliant light. Davo's scope was now rendered useless, since the flares spoilt the image it provided. But as flares drifted across the ridge, no movement could be seen amongst the rock spines that lined the feature. The enemy were good at not showing their cards too early. As the flares faded out, fresh flares burst above, keeping the light constant. The silent approach option was not what was on the cards, by the look of things. Those fuckers who withdrew from our assault last night were about to get another helping of carnage, chaos and mayhem on their new position.

Off to the north of the ridge, all hell was unleashed. A huge volume of red tracer came screaming in, smashing their targets. Some of the enemy scampered like ants from untenable positions, which were getting obliterated by the sheer weight of fire. As they fell back to rear positions, huge explosions smashed along the feature, shredding anyone caught in the open. This was the Royal Navy's contribution to the attack. MILAN missiles now joined in with the carnage, smashing bunkers, causing the roofs to cave in and crush those not brave enough to fall back through the naval gunfire. We had one hell of a ringside seat. The flares remained constant throughout the battle. Even Francis Ford Coppola couldn't create anything like this for Hollywood.

Lead companies of the Second Battalion came into the flare footprint. Advancing very spaced out. As they drew near the forward positions, they scampered about in pairs, dealing with the bunkers in turn. The thuds of their grenades were drowned out by the deafening soundtrack of their fire-support.

But as they got themselves sorted out round the bunkers, shells would smash all over their location, causing them to scatter like ants, into whatever cover was available. The Argentinians were not going quietly. Second Battalion would pay for any real estate they captured, that was very evident from our own experiences on Longdon. Once the counter-bombardment ceased, they emerged from whatever cover they had managed to find, and continued pushing forward.

Movement behind us broke our gaze, as Leighton and Zane scrambled up to us, covered in blankets and allsorts. "Here you go, guys," said Zane. "They don't smell too great, but they will do the job." He handed me a blanket, which was damp to the touch, and smelt absolutely vile, a mixture of mouldy cheese and body odour. But the cold had really settled in now, and the snowflakes were getting bigger, and were settling on the rocks around us. So I wrapped the blanket around me, which helped keep the wind off me if anything, the smell I would just have to put up with.

All wrapped up with smelly blankets and sleeping bags, we looked a right state. Who would think we were a professional army? More like conscripts on the retreat from Moscow. We went back to watching the battle raging before us. As the Second Battalion took ground, the Argentines would shell their lost positions, which made life difficult and progress slow. In the flare light, you could just make out small groups of enemy troops, moving back off Wireless Ridge, trying to make their way back to Moody Brook Barracks, which stood in the darkness, just outside the flare footprint.

Our artillery got wise to the retreat, as shells splashed amongst the withdrawing enemy. The artillery was wreaking havoc amongst them. Shells would land, and they would all dive to the ground, but every time it happened, less and less were getting back up. Some did manage to get out of the glare of our flares, but not many.

What happened next was one of the strangest things I'd ever seen. There was a large puff of smoke amongst the small houses on the outskirts of Port Stanley, and a white flash of light streaked off across Wireless Ridge, and out to sea at an amazing rate of knots. Whatever it was, and whether it was meant to be for our guys on the ridge, fuck knows! Strange.

More and more of the enemy were now falling back off Wireless Ridge, trying to make their escape through our artillery bombardment. It made for grim watching. The bombardment just shredded those caught in the open. Tracer from Second Battalion began to cut them down as well, since the reverse slope positions were now in our hands. Few flares were now in the air, and our grandstand view of the attack was reducing by the minute.

The flare light eventually faded altogether. As far as we were concerned, the show was over. Second Battalion were now taking care of their grim business in the dark. I pitied those Argentines foolish enough to still be holding out, it would not end well for them.

We turned in towards each other, and let out a small nervous chuckle at our own predicament. Cold, dirty, exhausted. There was still light off to our right, the battle for Tumbledown still in full swing. Flares drifted above its

225

peak, machineguns chattered, tracer flicking skywards, shells smashing into the summit. I didn't know much about the Scots Guards, but I felt sorry for those Argentines fighting for their lives, trying to keep a battalion of cold, tired Scotsmen from the chance of a bed and bath in Stanley.

"Right, that's it," Davo piped up. "I'm chinned. Let's get some kip, more adventures tomorrow." There were murmurs of agreement from the rest of us. We tucked ourselves into whatever crags in the alley walls there were. I was now glad of my new duvet jacket, and I understood why I'd just been given a blanket. Most of the lads only had their issued quilted suits, which were just not good enough in this weather. My own quilted trousers were shredded in my barrel bag, so I therefore had to suffer with cold legs for the night. My feet were frozen, but there was not much I could do about it, until daylight at least. Little sleep was to be had, despite how shattered I was. It was just too damn cold. I would drift off, and wake up a few seconds later, shivering my tits off. The soundtrack of Tumbledown was still in full force across the valley. The wind sweeping up the alley chilled us all to the bone.

Also playing on my shattered mind was what would be happening tomorrow. Planning for street fighting? I had images of Arnhem and Stalingrad in my head, when the front line couldn't be marked on a map, but was measured in who occupied which room, and which floor. Street fighting was savage at best; you could be right on top of your enemy, to the point where your weapons were just not effective in a confined space, such as a bedroom or basement. Hand-to-hand fighting would normally be what was needed to subdue an enemy in them tight spots, literally beating each other to death with whatever was to hand; furniture, fists, knives found in kitchen drawers, you name it. Artillery would be no good to us, once we broke into the town, since our observers could not ensure that friendly forces wouldn't be caught in their own barrages. What if the Argentines made a last stand in the sewers of Port Stanley? Many a tale of Stalingrad told you of grim skirmishes in the pitch-black shit-smeared tunnels under a cold shattered city.

What about snipers? A smashed-up town is ideal cover for the defender, a living nightmare for the attacker. I was confident in the ability of our snipers, but being a machine-gunner, I would certainly be on the menu for enemy sharpshooters. Many previous conflicts in cities generate stories of relaxing troops getting their heads shattered by the sniper's bullet. Just the one shot breeding panic amongst comrades, who would not be able to relax anywhere in the area. What have you got yourself into, Archie boy?

Tumbledown ceased to be a soundtrack. I only hoped it had ended in our favour. It sounded pretty intense at some points through the night, as I shivered under my stinking blanket, trying to rest. I pulled the blanket from my face and peered down the alley, to where what was left of our Company was trying to sleep. Some stood in small groups, smoking and chatting. Some had even got their hexi burners out, and had started cooking. Dawn was on its way, as daylight began to make an appearance off to the east. I looked over to my right, and caught Jamie starting to fidget under his captured sleeping bag. Keeping his head covered, he cocked his right leg in the air, and let off a really squeaky fart that echoed down the alley, causing some lads huddled around a burner to look up at us, and begin to chuckle. He then sat bolt upright. "I think someone has taken a shit in my mouth." Charming. To be fair, he had a point; it had been a while since any of us had brushed our teeth. "What time is it?"

I couldn't be arsed to look at my watch. "Daytime."

He grinned. "Hey, I do the jokes, and you do the cooking." With the blanket draped over my shoulders, I went about getting breakfast on the go. Most of the

Company were up and moving, all with the same thing in mind. I stood up and let out an almighty stretch. I climbed to the top of the alley, and looked out towards Wireless Ridge and Port Stanley. The street lights were slowly going out, as daylight became established. I could see clearly the Second Battalion milling about on their positions. Apart from the wind, all was quiet. Peering down at the base of the bowl, I could see what I could only guess was C Company, beginning to move off in the direction of Wireless. They marched in two columns, which began to climb over the saddle that separated Longdon from Wireless. Further off to the right, some distance away, was the shattered remains of Moody Brook Barracks, their objective. I went back to tend to breakfast, which I had neglected. By the look of things, Jamie had taken up the role of chef.

As we sat there and ate, there was a commotion at the bottom of the alley. Justin and Dale were moving from group to group, and as they moved on, the groups were hugging and backslapping each other. Davo had woken, and sat up scratching his head. I could see his eyes narrow, to focus on what the hell was going on.

Justin and Dale reached us, all smiles. "The Argentines have called for a ceasefire," said Justin. "Second Battalion are moving through Moody Brook now, and are pushing up to the racecourse. Make safe your weapons, enjoy your breakfast."

They turned and made their way back down the alley, Dale giving me a wink as they left. Numb was an understatement. Davo put his face in his hands, his shoulders bouncing as he began to sob. No more killing. I could see Jamie's eyes had glazed over, and tears began to run down his face, as he gave me a beaming smile. We didn't speak for a while; we just sat there, in our own thoughts, tears rolling down our filthy faces. No more killing. No one needed to die today, no one.

CHAPTER 14: Port Stanley

We made our weapons safe. Still loaded, but in order to fire them, you had to cock a round into the breach before they would work. It all felt like the end of an exercise. I unloaded the Gimpy completely, and ensured the working parts of the gun were forward, then placed the belt back on. We packed away our kit, and waited for Dale to call us down into the RAP, hopefully for the last time. We just sat there grinning at each other. No gunfire, no shelling, no screaming, no dying, it felt fucking wonderful.

The word came. We all clambered to our feet, and shuffled down out of the horrible world of rock and shit. We skirted right, back around towards the RAP, everyone in single file, purely out of habit, both hands on our weapons, since it could all go wrong with the Second Battalion, hard on the heels of those Argentines legging it back into Port Stanley.

The RAP looked a lot different this morning. Our dead and wounded had been back-loaded, probably to Teal. The enemy dead were nowhere to be seen, either buried or back-loaded also. The prisoners were being marched back to Estancia, no doubt. Sadness hit me square in the face. All those guys, theirs and ours that had been killed or wounded, so close to the end, it was so sad. We noticed everyone was just milling about in the open, not seeking shelter amongst the boulders and rocks, through fear of shelling. Some of those gathered had removed their helmets, clipping them onto their belt kit.

Justin and Dale walked amongst us, wearing their maroon berets, and shaking hands with us all. It felt rather bizarre. It was only a couple of days ago, when they were shaking our hands prior to the attack. Everyone began putting their berets on. I fished mine out of my smock inside pocket. It was in a bit of a state, damp from my own sweat, covered in bits of fluff, and the kind of random crap that gathers in one's pockets after a while. I gave it a good shake, picked the worst of the fluff and crap off it, and placed it onto my head. There is a certain way the British soldier wears their beret. If you wear it as the regulations say, you look like Benny Hill, and so you have to push your luck a bit with regards to style. In our Battalion, we would have the bottom tip of our cap badge between the left eye and ear, so you didn't look like a right wally, when it came to being in the public eye. Beret firmly on my head, I clipped my helmet to the back of my webbing.

"Prepare to move," Dale called out to us. I didn't want to march into town with the duvet jacket on, so I scrambled out of my kit, and placed my fighting gear back on. Jamie stuffed the jacket through the yolk straps between my back and the top of my pouches. I'd lost track of my barrel bag, and there was not much I could do about it now.

Our Company began to shuffle forward in two columns towards Wireless Ridge. A Company had already moved off from their position, and were making their way to Moody Brook Barracks. Gimpy over my right shoulder, I followed the column over the saddle that separated Wireless from Longdon. In the distance, near the water's edge, I could see columns of troops marching along. There was talk of a possible minefield, but this didn't slow us down in the slightest. We were heading in the direction of Moody Brook, which was near the edge of the bay that Port Stanley sits on. The barracks was the home of a small commando garrison when the Argentines invaded. It was destroyed in the initial invasion; luckily the commandos had abandoned it, sometime the day before.

We encountered a number of enemy dead on our way towards the barracks, shredded by our artillery as they fled towards Port Stanley. We gave them a token glance, and then moved on. We'd seen enough of death. We just wanted to get it over with and go home.

As we drew alongside the barracks, we saw it was just a burnt-out wreck of a site. Some of our lads, not too sure which company, were dealing with a couple of prisoners, who must have sheltered there after the onslaught of the night before. Our lads finished searching them, gave them a cigarette, and walked with them onto the tarmac road that connected the barracks to the town. Truly remarkable, no rough treatment, both sides walking down the road, smoking cigarettes, relieved it was over. No one had to die today. As I made my way onto the tarmac, it felt like a gift from the gods. Up until now, it was just cold rain-soaked peat or tussock grass beating up my feet, but now we had tarmac, it felt great. The local council had its work cut out. The road was covered in all sorts of crap; mud, blood, ammunition, weapons, bloody bandages, spent bullet casings, all the clutter that comes with battle. It was all over the shop. We just stepped over it and moved on. We encountered more enemy dead on the road. Someone had taken the time to cover them up with some corrugated sheeting, their boots poking out of one end, such a shame.

We were told to hold up. We just all bunched up, pushed over to the right side of the road, and sat down. Word came down the line that we were to give the Argentines some breathing space as they left the town, and gathered on the airfield further to the east. Some would argue it was unwise to give an enemy such room to move, but orders were orders.

As we sat there, a steady stream of what could only be our Second Battalion were marching past on their way into town. So why had we been told to stay put? I stood up and looked down the road. It quickly dawned on me that Port Stanley was in bad shape. A couple of buildings were on fire, all sorts of gear strewn all over the road. It no longer gave you the feel of an oasis, as it had when viewed from Longdon. It was now probably nothing more than a ransacked fishing town.

Word came down the line for us to move. Everyone got to their feet, and adjusted their loads. We then shuffled off down the road towards town, and very soon we were veering off to the right, onto the racecourse. Hardly Kempton Park, the Argentines had trashed it. The gun line was established there, loads of artillery pieces pointing towards the mountains, with crude earthworks and turfs piled up around them, in an attempt to conceal them and protect their crews. Empty shell cases were strewn all over the place, crates of ammunition were piled up behind the guns, open to the elements. I'm sure members of the Royal Artillery upon seeing this shambles of a gun line would have a heart attack at such disarray. Trenches next to their positions, which I assumed were filled to the brim with water for the gun crews. The tents alongside were just rain-soaked canvas hovels. Did they sleep in the houses? Or just slum it the best they could out in the open?

We made our way through the gun line towards the first cluster of bungalows. Small trampled hedgerows separated the gun line and the town, and it was here we were told to go firm. It started to rain. Some of the guys got their ponchos out and pitched them up, along whatever fence lines were available. Others got brews on the go, cigarettes were smoked and jokes were cracked, usual shit.

A few of the lads ventured towards the bungalows, and peered through the windows. They then turned around, shrugged their shoulders, and made their way back to us. Word soon passed around not to break into any of the houses, due to possible booby traps, and we had to wait for engineers to clear them. Moans and groans swept through us like wildfire, with certain anonymous voices commenting on officers merely playing for time, whilst they looked for the best beds and baths. It did cross my mind, don't get me wrong, but to be honest, as long as we eventually got out of the weather, I didn't give a monkey's where I slept. I'd lost track of Jamie and I went in search of him. When I found him, he was under a poncho, hot chocolate ready to go and a cheeky grin on his face. "Took your time," he teased. "I got bored of waiting."

I scrambled out of my fighting gear and slipped the duvet jacket over my smock, sliding underneath to join him. We had to stay put for most of the day, as engineers ensured the bungalows we wanted to occupy were cleared of booby traps and the like. Out on the road, columns of commandos with their heavy packs had made their way out of the mountains, and were trudging into Port Stanley. They were all full of smiles, and we would exchange professional nods to each other. There was nothing more than professional rivalry between us and them, only the minority of clowns would make it out to be any deeper than that. The commandos had their fair share of misery on this fucking island, and to top it off, they'd slogged it out with Bergens. Our Bergens had yet to be brought forward from Estancia, but if we were indoors tonight, it shouldn't be too much of a discomfort.

Word come round that the buildings were clear and we could now occupy them. The owners were staying with friends further into town, in order to make room for their liberators, bloody nice of them. Dale rallied the Company and gave us a heads up. "Right lads, I will show you to your accommodation, a platoon at a time, but I must warn you now, they are trashed. The Argentines have shit and pissed everywhere, and it looks like they've burgled the place as well." For fuck sake, what was their thing with shitting everywhere? "4 Platoon," he ordered, "get your gear and follow me."

As they were led off to their bungalows, Davo ordered 5 Platoon to gear up and get ready. We could hear 4 Platoon cursing out loud at the state of their dwellings, which made the rest of the Company chuckle. Don't know why we were so smug, we had yet to see ours.

We made our way over, and Davo led us through the first row of buildings to our bungalow, which from the outside didn't look too bad. The owners must have had small children, since there was a swing and slide, plus random children's toys strewn about the garden. We set foot inside. The stench of shit and piss hit us square in the face. It was all over the floor, even on the kitchen units, why would you do this? It's just not civilized, war or not. Davo had seen enough. "Right, everyone get outside, drop your gear off, we need to blitz it room by room."

We all stripped off our gear outside, down to just shirts, preparing to do some serious housework. Davo spammed Jamie and I with collecting up all the shit that was literally everywhere. Being the newest Private soldiers in the platoon, this was our chore. Leighton and Zane grinned at us menacingly under their bushy gringo 'tashes, since it clearly wasn't going to be them on poo-picking duty. Their faces dropped when Davo spammed them with clearing all the shit-smeared furniture out of the bungalow, and putting it in the garden. They glared at us, but we avoided their hard stares, and suddenly found hunting for turds very interesting. Davo put others to task, clearing out the remainder of the rubbish strewn all over the place, plus sweeping and mopping, etc. How bizarre was this whole experience? This time yesterday, we were getting shelled on a mountainside, and today, we were sweeping and mopping out a bungalow. Hollywood gets war films wrong every time.

The whole effort took the better part of a couple of hours. Our bungalow was clear but almost bare, since a lot of the furniture stacked up in the garden was not fit for use. This actually worked in our favour; we had more floor space to get everyone in and settled. The whole place now reeked with bleach, which burned the nostrils, but we were enjoying luxury. A kitchen allowed us to eat in a human fashion. A bathroom with a toilet allowed us to get ourselves clean. Clean!

There was a knock at the front door, which felt weird, and in strolled Dale with Justin, doing the rounds. "Blimey fellas," Dale chuckled, "very plush." We were rather proud of our efforts. They had a sneaky nose about our place, nodding in approval.

We knew what was coming next; they were just hedging their bets on which platoon to live with. Justin got to the point first. "Got any room for us?"

Davo looked at the floor, shaking his head, chuckling. "Yes sir, let me do a bit of a reshuffle, and we will get you in." Davo would now be known to the platoon as Basil.

As Dale left with Justin to carry on their inspections, he let us know the Bergens would be dropped onto the racecourse by Chinook. We bundled out with just our weapons, and as we made our way through the garden, you could hear the drumming thud of helicopter rotor blades getting louder.

We gathered on the edge of the racecourse, as the huge heavily loaded beast hovered, about a hundred metres away. Beneath it was a huge cargo net, full to capacity with Bergens and kitbags. Just as the net made contact with the ground, whatever was used to connect it to the helicopter came loose, and the huge bundle thudded on the turf. The Chinook remained in the hover and turned to the left, showing us its tailgate, then landing just behind the bundle. Amid the din of rotors and engines, not to mention the monstrous draught that almost pushed you over if you were not braced for it, the tailgate lowered to expose two figures, one of which was the loadmaster. He got the ramp

240

as he wanted it and then gave us the thumbs up. Dale returned the gesture, and with a wave of his right arm led us forward towards the bundle and the aircraft. The draught from the rotors intensified as we walked closer, in a half-crouch kind of waddle. As we got to the bundle, Dale placed his hand on the left shoulder of a number of us, including me. Pointing at the remainder to deal with the Bergens, he waved us on towards the Chinook.

The noise was a deafening whine as the engines continued to run. As we got closer, the surface water of the racecourse stung our faces, as we made our way to the tailgate. The shower was short lived, since we soon began to get the benefits of being behind the aircraft. The engines dried us off almost instantly, and for a short while it was a wonderful feeling. I quickly recognised the second person on the tailgate; it was Phil, our Company Quartermaster Sergeant. I hadn't seen him since San Carlos. He shook hands with Dale, who turned, waving me onto the ramp. Phil didn't waste any time or fuel talking to me, he just handed me Bergens, kitbags, ammo, rations, jerry cans of water, plus other random crap. I merely spun round and handed them to the guy behind me, who happened to be Dale. He had arranged a human chain to quickly get all the gear off the aircraft as quickly as possible.

In this fashion, we quickly emptied the Chinook. As we were waved off the ramp, Phil was using a torch to check the inside of the aircraft, just in case we had left anything behind. Happy we hadn't missed anything, he then shook hands with the loadmaster, and joined us crouching over our kit. The ramp went up, and the whole pitch of the engine noise increased, as the huge machine began to climb into the air once again, its rotor downdraught pressing us hard into the kit we had just unloaded. The din began to subside, the Chinook on its way back into the mountains for its next task.

For the next hour or so, it was all hands to the pump, getting our Company stores over to the bungalows. 4 Platoon had taken a lot of casualties, so therefore had the most room in which to get our stores under cover, out of the elements. Once all the humping and dumping was complete, we shouldered our Bergens and made our way back to our little palace. Our bungalow became cluttered with kit, getting pulled from our Bergens as we got ourselves comfortable.

Davo had given Company Headquarters the master bedroom, which made space in the living room a bit tight, but we managed. I unrolled my sleeping bag and sat on it, getting totally stripped off. I then stood up and whipped on a clean pair of boxer shorts, giving my body a bit of a once over. Back at home, it could be safely said that I was somewhat tubbier than the majority of our platoon. Not unfit, just not very toned. But my ribcage was very prominent now, all my excess weight burnt off during our series of marches, and living on rations. My legs were well-defined, since they had received a big workout TABbing everywhere. I had sores on my hips and the base of my back, from where my webbing had rubbed. My feet didn't look too clever. Not in pain or anything, they'd just not seen the light of day for some time.

Pretty much everyone in the living room had the same idea as me. For a male civilian, being crammed into a room with a load of semi-naked men could cause some discomfort, but we were well past giving a fuck, considering what we had all been through in the last couple of weeks. Once I was content I wasn't going to keel over and die anytime soon, I treated myself to a fresh pair of socks and a clean shirt, my trainers on for the time being.

For a while, I just lay on my sleeping bag, as the lads got themselves sorted. After a time, the chaos that had dominated the room subsided, ending with rather content men lying on their bags smoking, picking their noses or having a scratch. The room now had the aroma of toothpaste, foot powder, cigarette smoke, farts and feet, the usual odour of a barrack block. Jamie, who was pitched up to my right, was out for the count. He was open-mouthed, like he was trying to catch flies, snoring his head off. I sat up and looked around my immediate area for something to throw at him, but to no avail. Someone had AC/DC beating out a track on a tape recorder in one of the bedrooms, which got my foot tapping, but the constant beating of drums was making me doze off.

What could only have been a few minutes of sleep had actually been an hour or so. I felt a nudge, opened one eye, and Jamie was sat up looking at Justin and Dale, stood in the centre of the room. As I sat up, I noticed the whole room was crammed with everyone from the Company. Something was afoot. "Gentlemen," Justin said. He had our attention. "The Argentine forces have formally surrendered." Teary eyes and beaming smiles filled the room in an instant. "General Moore took the surrender about ten minutes ago. The Argentine General Menendez has signed a document stating that Argentina will cease all operations on both East and West Falkland. It's over. Congratulations and very well done."

Fantastic, no one else had to die. We could all see Justin starting to well up, and when he grabbed Dale in a big bear hug, we all cheered. It let the tension out of the room. We all stood up, shaking hands with each other, tears rolling down all our faces. The moment was just too nice an occasion to really give a toss about the macho image we liked to portray. The war was over, and it meant we could go home soon, see our parents, our children, our wives and girlfriends. Fucking brilliant. Once all the hugging and backslapping had run its course, Dale wiped the tears from his eyes and called for order. We quietened down. "Right lads, we've now got a rather pissed off defeated army sat out at the airport, who still have their weapons and ammo with them. The commandos have been tasked with disarming them in the morning, and then the Argentines will be put to task with clearing up this town, since they made the bloody mess." Some tittering could be heard with nods of agreement. "Our Company has been tasked with clearing up the racecourse, using prisoners to do the donkey work. You are there to guard them, not talk about the football, and just make sure they behave and do the clear up, understood?" We all nodded, I'd forgotten about the football. "Right then," he continued, "get some rest. I want at least two people awake at any one time, so we can respond to any sudden dramas in the night. Have a fag and a brew by the front door, whatever, just be awake. Anyone fucks this up, their entire platoon will move out onto the racecourse, is that clear?"

A chorus of "yes sir" was heard across the room. No one wanted to sleep outside anymore. With that, the other platoons departed, and we got ourselves settled. No one appeared to be in a rush to get some sleep, many still high on the surrender news, me included.

Jamie and I went into the kitchen, to see if the kettle worked. It did, bonus. The plumbing was a bit ropey and the water was just a trickle out of the taps, so we used what water we had in our webbing. With brews in hand, we made our way to the front door. Davo, Leighton and Zane were on the porch. Davo had his rifle across his knees, whilst the other two hoods were trying to tune in a little radio they had found, probably trying to get the football. These two goons frowned more and more as they tried to get a signal, and their gringo 'tashes made them look all the more sinister. "You okay guys?" piped up Davo, once he realised we were there.

"Yeah, not bad at all," Jamie answered. "Just glad it's over."

Davo grinned and nodded, and focused on the rifle in his lap. "You lads did well up there." He pointed off into the distance. Wireless Ridge was in plain view, and in the fading light, you could just make out the summit of Longdon peering over the top. It looked a million miles away. "All we need to do now is get this town back into shape, and get the hell out of here."

The gruesome twosome dropped the radio on the floor. Leighton stamped on it and stormed inside, whilst Zane remained, putting a cigarette between his lips and lighting it. "Fucking thing," he mumbled. Davo looked at him, as he blew his first plume of smoke into the air. Then Davo looked at me, before looking back to his weapon, shoulders bouncing as he stifled a chuckle. Zane was a horrible looking bastard, you would not want him playing Santa Claus at your kids' party, but up on Longdon he was solid as a rock. When Dale had pushed me back up to join the platoon after I had fallen in that trench, Zane had got to grips with me, and had given me an update of what was going on and where, which goes to show that Private soldiers can read the battle as it unfolds around them. Me personally, I wouldn't have received Man of the Match with regards to the battle, since for the majority of the assault, I was just a fat sweaty mess, and not entirely sure of what was going on. Zane would get my vote.

Cheering could be heard further into town, as news of the surrender spread. As happy as I was that this whole terrible episode would nearly be over for us, I couldn't help but feel sadness for those who were not here to share in the celebrations. I didn't envy the Argentines either, as

247

they made their way to the airport, awaiting processing. I didn't know if they had enough shelter tonight, but at least they were alive to complain about such conditions. I reflected on some of the enemy dead we encountered on Longdon. It really hit home how brutally them guys met their deaths. Our boys had destroyed those positions and them men with extreme violence. Bodies and bunkers riddled with bullet holes, half-naked men caught clambering out of tents, and sleeping bags splintered by grenades and bayonets, as our guys rolled through their positions. Brave defenders crushed by their own bunkers as anti-tank missiles collapsed them. Terrified conscripts put to the bayonet in the horrific night-fighting amongst the rocks. A truly grim experience for both sides.

As I made my way back into the bungalow, most of the lads had settled down for the night, quietly chatting away. Jamie was already in his bag, having a good old pick of his nose before turning in for the night. I stripped down to just my boxer shorts and clambered into my bag. It felt so nice not to have to wear all of your clothing. The sleeping bag felt huge on me. I didn't smell too great, but that could all be dealt with tomorrow. AC/DC had called it a night by this point as well, since its owner had probably either turned in, or been told to turn it off. No doubt in the night, I would be woken for a stint keeping watch at the front door, but I would just deal with that when I got a shove.

The shove came. I felt it was my turn to stand watch. As I pulled the sleeping bag from my drool-smeared face, I could see it was early dawn. People were dressed and milling around, with cups of tea and cigarettes on the go. I leaned over to Jamie, who was doing his bootlaces up. "Good morning handsome," he said, "want a brew?"

I sat up, fearful of a swift reprisal for missing my turn on watch. None came. "Why did no one wake me?" I mumbled.

"Fuck knows, no one woke me either. I heard some of the lads chatting and smoking by the door all night, maybe they couldn't sleep."

I clambered out of the bag and sat on it cross-legged, just trying to tune in. Some of the guys were still sound asleep, which made me feel more relaxed. Dale walked in through the front door fully dressed, and called for everyone's attention. Those asleep were nudged awake. "Guys, the commandos have started processing the prisoners. Don't expect to see any with us for a few hours. Take this time to get your admin sorted. I want to see clean shaven faces, plus polish on boots. The media are going to be around here soon, like flies around a turd. So don't show yourselves up. If they ask you about Longdon, refer them to me or the OC for the clean edited version, understood?" We all nodded. "Engineers and some artillery punters are gonna be here soon, to ensure the gun line can be moved, so don't go fucking about with their artillery. Some may be booby trapped or still loaded from the other night."

He made his way into the master bedroom. I perched up on my knees at the end of my bag, and began to rifle through my Bergen. I rubbed my hand over my face. I could no longer get away with not shaving. It had been a few days since my last flirt with a razor. My boxers and socks were fresh from yesterday, so I got dressed, and with my shaving kit, I made my way outside. Some of the lads were stripped to the waist around a saucepan of hot water on top of an oil drum, scraping hair and old cam cream off their faces for the first time in days. As they shaved, the transformation I watched was amazing, changing from rough grizzled combat veterans back to young fresh-faced lads, in a few strokes of a razor. I looked twelve most of the time, and at the moment I just looked like a twelve-year-old with too much bum fluff, so the shaving effect wouldn't be too much of a change. Once a gap presented itself for me to squeeze into, I got on with my ablutions. Once all sorted and teeth brushed, I got fully dressed and awaited our workforce of Argentine prisoners.

The platoon was all shaved and polished, by the time our workforce arrived. A small group of commandos had marched the prisoners in some kind of military order up to our meeting point. Dale exchanged a few words with the commando escorts, who then left the prisoners under our charge for the remainder of the day. He had arranged for some of our guys to get a couple of captured trucks up to the racecourse, in order to tow the guns out onto the beach, so they were out of the way.

He assigned groups of prisoners to the platoons for the day's tasks. 4 Platoon's prisoners would move all the live ammunition to the beach, for collection by the Royal Engineers. Their prisoners had a full day's work ahead of them, because there was fuck loads of it. Our platoon's prisoners would get the guns hitched up to the trucks, and get them off the racecourse. Once done, our prisoners would then help 6 Platoon's prisoners, clearing all the remaining crap from the racecourse that didn't belong there. It was going to be a long cold day.

The original plan for 4 Platoon's prisoners soon went to rat shit, due to the fact that there was far too much ammo for the prisoners to shift on their own. There was tons of the stuff, most of it artillery shells. I had never seen such vast quantities of ammo in one place. It made the ammo stacked up at San Carlos on the first day look poxy in comparison. Our gunners probably dreamed of having such vast amounts available to them, certainly during this campaign. If the Argies had really gone to town on us as we hunkered down on Longdon, they could have really given us a good hiding. But what had been the quality of the gun crews and their observers, conscript or regular? I would like to think that regular gunners would have given us a real run for our money, and maybe kept a tidier gun line. The whole Company and all the prisoners got to grips with the ammo, just to get it cleared. It took hours. Every time we moved to a new gun position, we would have to wait for engineers to ensure the ammo was safe, before clearing it. It was late afternoon, by the time the majority of the ammo was shifted over to the beach. We left 4 Platoon and their prisoners to finish off the last couple of positions, while our prisoners and those of 6 Platoon went back to the original tasks.

Our prisoners' job was pretty straightforward. The trucks all had towing hooks, but we didn't have the means to connect them to the guns. Dale came over with some ratchet straps he must have scrounged from somewhere, and dropped them at our prisoners' feet. "Don't worry about the lawn. Just get the guns dragged out of here."

One by one, we helped our prisoners to literally strap the trailing legs of the first gun to the back of the truck, our driver giving it plenty of gas as we dragged it off the racecourse, the truck ploughing as it went. Well, it couldn't make this bloody position any worse. The Argentines had been long past caring about the lawn.

We were in the process of connecting up the second gun, when we heard some old fella in a flat cap and Barbour jacket come over, ranting and raving about what we had done to his precious furlong. He demanded to speak to those in command, and we pointed him in the direction of Dale, who was stood near the bungalows, having a brew with the OC. The old guy stormed away in their direction, leaving us to continue ploughing the guns over to the beach. Fuck knows what he said to them, the ungrateful fuck, but neither Justin nor Dale rushed over to reprimand us.

With the ammo and guns shifted, all we had left to do was help 6 Platoon's prisoners clear the remainder of random crap, scattered all over the shop. Dale got bored with the whole enterprise by early evening, and told us it could wait 'til the morning. The commando escorts for our prisoners were already waiting on the road for them. As our prisoners made their way over to the road, some had the cheek to ask some of us for cigarettes. What harm could it do? Zane surprised me the most, and gave them a whole packet with his thumbs up. They waved goodbye to us, and got into some kind of order on the road, wandering off with their escorts back to the airport. The prisoners weren't a bad bunch, to be fair. They did as they were told without complaint, and chatted away in Spanish, with the occasional chuckle and a high five here and there. To be honest, if they were happy, there was probably less chance of a revolt. They just wanted to go home, me too. During the course of that day, shifting ammo with the Gimpy slung across my back was a royal pain in the arse, but Dale had insisted we remained armed. The racecourse was now two-thirds clear, just the remaining shite to clear in the morning. We wandered back to our bungalows for a well-deserved brew, and something to eat.

The usual admin chaos ensued. Talk of a church service the following afternoon was doing the rounds, which wasn't a problem, since it wouldn't be long before we got the job on the racecourse finished. There was what appeared to be media, loitering between the bungalows, snapping away with their cameras, and trying to strike up conversation with whoever was outside having a fag. I played it safe and stayed in the bungalow. I would only drop myself in the shit for expressing an opinion that would make headline news. Better for them to interview officers, who could dazzle them with long complicated words they learned at university and Sandhurst. Archie from Portsmouth, with his cat-sat-on-the-mat schooling and vocabulary, would not make for good reading at the best of times, so I kept out of the media's way.

In the kitchen, there was commotion and the rattling of pots and pans. I peered around the door, and could see Leighton and Zane with their sleeves rolled up, getting stuck into some serious cooking. On the counter next to them was a large cardboard box of rations, with gold tins of various grub scattered all over the place. The pot they were stirring and heating was massive, as they continued to pour random sludge from various tins into it. I ducked back out of sight, in case they caught me and put me on washing-up duty. I went back over to where my sleeping bag was, un-slung the gun and parked my arse. Jamie was oblivious to my arrival, as he was routing through his Bergen for something. I gave him a nudge, which made him jump. "What are Pinky and Perky up to in the kitchen?" I asked him.

"I think they are doing an 'all in' for the platoon." An 'all in' is a soldier's term for mass feeding. Instead of us all trying to cook our individual meals, all over the bungalow and garden, it made sense to exploit the kitchen facilities at hand, and feed everyone at once. Nice idea. We couldn't use the hexi burners indoors, because the fumes from the tablets are poisonous in the right quantities. Before long,

Zane peered around the door, announcing dinner was ready. The usual jibes about food poisoning echoed around the room, but we all lined up for our share. I wasn't going to complain. I couldn't be arsed to go out into the cold and cook my own anyway. The loitering media would only ruin my appetite. As I arrived at the front of the queue, they scooped my helping into my mess tin, and it was then they broadsided me with the pan-washing after dinner. Bastards. They told me to bring my girlfriend to dry up, indicating Jamie. I chuckled, which caught his attention. It quickly dawned on him what they were saying. He quickly had an answer for them. "I will have you know gentlemen, that I pitch, and my fair lady here catches." The gruesome twosome just rolled their eyes, and reminded us we were on washing-up detail after scoff, and less of the lip.

   The food wasn't at all bad. It was a stew of sorts, just a random selection of meat, veg, and a shit load of gravy thrown in, with a job lot of hard tack biscuits chucked in to thicken it up. It was hot, it was simple, and it filled the hole. Davo asked out loud what was for pudding. Leighton informed him that it was whatever we could find for ourselves in the boxes. You just can't beat this type of customer service. I enjoyed the stew that much, that I went up for another helping, which started a slow trickle of diners to do the same. It wasn't long before the large pot was as good as bare, and I could commence the washing up. There wasn't any washing-up liquid, but I found a semi-clean rag under the sink, and made sure the water was hot enough to do the job. Jamie wandered in, and sat on the counter next to the sink. "You'd think your shit job stint would have died with Danny, wouldn't you?"

It didn't get the giggle he was after. I didn't find it funny. I just looked into the water. Danny had been leant against a bunker, face smashed in by tracer, arm almost ripped off, his torso riddled with machinegun fire. I'm sure I wasn't the only soldier that has ever thought about their own demise in the heat of battle; guns blazing with an awesome soundtrack, as your last action destroys the enemy. I had watched Danny die the other night. It wasn't in a blaze of glory. He was pulverized beyond recognition in a fraction of a second, by a machine-gunner who was mutually supporting the bunker. Well sited, very deadly, nothing more. It is very cliché to think that it should be Danny stood over you when you are badly wounded, because that's the way it works on exercise. It didn't go that way at all the other night. Before we knew it, we had a lance corporal as platoon commander, with whatever Private soldiers had the balls to step up, and take command of the chaos in the cold darkness. It's true what they say; you are just one bullet away from being in charge.

I felt a hand on my shoulder, which snapped me out of it. "Sorry mate," Jamie grinned, "bad timing." I smiled, it wasn't his fault, it was just business. I set about scrubbing the pan. Without washing-up liquid, I wasn't really getting anywhere. He routed through a few drawers and found a tea towel, so we just wiped the pan dry, and in the process removed the remains of the stew, done. We went back into the living room, to find the lads just lying about, chatting quietly and smoking. Considering the conflict was as good as over, it felt more of an anti-climax. I had the impression we could not go home until Stanley was back in some sort of order. I got undressed and climbed into my bag, and pondered in my thoughts. I just wanted to go home.

Next morning came with no fanfare, just the usual routine of ablutions and feeding. Once shaved, dressed and fed, I made my way outside, just to get out of the way, since there wasn't much room in there, with everyone trying to do the same thing. We had another problem on our hands now. I'm not sure if it was Zane and Leighton's cooking, but in the night, a few of the lads had to make a dash to the toilet. The plumbing couldn't cope with the volume of customers, so some had to dash out into the cold night in just underwear, and shit in the bushes at the end of the garden. Some hadn't made it. Toilet roll was a bit of a scarce commodity in Port Stanley, and if all the troops crammed into it suffered with the shits, things could get rather grim around here, very quickly. I wasn't feeling the effects as of yet, but Jamie admitted feeling rather ropey. He realised it when he went to conduct his morning fart, and all of a sudden lost confidence in the outcome, having to dash away to avoid a disaster.

Dale and Justin returned from their morning meeting with the CO, and gave us the news that our church service was postponed twenty-four hours, since it became apparent that the entire Battalion wasn't faring any better than us. The clearance of the racecourse would continue. Our group of prisoners arrived once again, and got to work clearing up what was left around the gun positions. They found it a source of entertainment, when their armed guards would have to scamper over hedges at the sides, to allow the Devil within to leave their bodies in liquid form. If it made the prisoners laugh, then morale would remain high, for them anyway.

On the beach, a number of fires were started, so a lot of the rubbish could be burnt. Dale reminded us over and over again to ensure there was no ammo hidden in the mouldy tents, or random boxes and crates. No one wanted to get blown up after the surrender, so we were thorough. We took a bit of a breather now and again, so our guys could dash off for a shit, and the prisoners could have a smoke. Beached next to the huge piles of ammo was a landing craft, like we had used to get into San Carlos. There were guys all over it, putting the ammo onboard. Word got round that the engineers were going to take it out to sea, and throw the ammo over the side, since there was far too much of it to be destroyed safely. I dreaded to think how much all that ammo cost, and all it was destined for was the seabed.

We were joined by teenage kids from Port Stanley, who were walking around with big flasks, dishing out the contents to our lads. When it came to my turn, I found it was tea, very sweet tea, with enough sugar in it to make a fly diabetic. I wasn't going to complain, I savoured every moment of it. Our prisoners had made themselves scarce, whilst we had the tea. They sat at the side of the road, sharing a cigarette or two. Maybe after occupying Port Stanley for three months, they knew the chances of them getting a cup of tea were as good as zero.

Zane eventually took a cup over to the prisoners, who accepted it gratefully. After all, it was a bloody cold day, and weather reports indicated it wasn't going to get any warmer. Everyone had stopped what they were doing to watch his random act. He looked like an axe murderer at the best of times, but had displayed random acts of kindness on more than one occasion. The teenagers had looked at each other, shrugging shoulders, when one of the girls walked over to the prisoners, and started dishing out the brew. Sheepishly, her friends followed her example. Some of the lads walked across the road, and started giving out cigarettes. I felt a huge swelling of emotion brew up inside me, and I tried my hardest to keep it in, but my eyes gave it away. I caught the gaze of Leighton, who just nodded and winked at me, nothing more needed to be said. No one else needed to die here.

Zane came over to where we were standing. He lit himself a cigarette, and looked out over the harbour, deep in thought. Davo piped up. "Getting soft in your old age, mate."

Zane blew out a mouthful of smoke, and looked at the floor. "They're just kids, not much older than him," he said, pointing at me. Davo glanced at me, and then nodded in agreement. A lot of our prisoners were fucking young, fresh out of school if a day. I was young, but I was in a far better position than they were, better trained in all our platoon weapons, and better fed, although you wouldn't believe it by the look of me at that moment. I was better paid. My bank credits would be looking rather flush upon my return home. I was physically fitter, though the TAB across this bloody island would lead you to believe otherwise. All in all, I was a better soldier than those poor sods sat at the roadside.

Dale snapped us all out of it. "Right, you bunch of soft twats. Before we start playing football in no man's land, get this fucking racecourse sorted, snap to it." Flasks empty, the teenagers waved goodbye, as we escorted our prisoners back onto the racecourse, to finish up the tasks for today. It was looking a damn sight better than it did yesterday morning, apart from the odd random clutter to be collected and burned. All that remained to be done was filling in holes and putting the turfs back. The prisoners understood what needed to be done. Some of them knew basic English, and got on with the gardening. We huddled together, trying to keep warm, hoping the girls would come back with fresh flasks and warm smiles.

We noticed Justin doing the rounds with the moaning old gentleman from yesterday, inspecting all the positions where the guns were placed. Justin was making notes, which he would probably have to pass on to whoever deals with ruined racecourses. As he drew near, we could still hear the old twat rambling on about how we caused more damage, towing the guns to the beach. Zane flicked his fag butt into one of the waterlogged holes, right in front of the old fart, who looked up red-faced, on the verge of rage. Zane glared right back at him. Justin rolled his eyes and gave Dale a look, with a flick of his head in Zane's direction. Justin ushered Mr Angry to the next position. Dale came level with Zane, and gave him a raised eyebrow. Zane capitulated. "Fair enough, I'll behave."

Dale gave him a pat on the back. "Chill out, mate. Let's just get this done, and get the fuck out of here. Ungrateful bastards, the lot of 'em." Situation defused, we went about keeping warm, and watching the landscape gardening, Argentine style. After a while, the prisoners had done as much as they physically could with regards to sorting out the turfs on each gun position. It still looked a bloody mess, but that was about as good as it was going to get, until people could come in with some serious machinery, and resurface the whole damn thing.

We allowed the prisoners one last cigarette, before they made the long cold trek back to the airport. As they wandered off, it quickly dawned on us that they no longer had an escort. No one appeared to give a toss. I doubted very much that these young exhausted lads were going to kick off, now they had handed over all their weapons and ammo to us.

We wandered back towards the bungalows in dribs and drabs, with not much else to do for the time being. The remainder of the Battalion, plus other units living in

Stanley, were dealing with tidying up parts of town with their prisoner labour, so we didn't feel the need to volunteer our services, and sought the warmth of our accommodation.

As Jamie and I drew near our bungalow, I could hear shouting, and the clattering of furniture. We turned the corner to see Phil and Dale in the midst of a full-on domestic with another man, who was throwing the stacked-up shitty furniture all over the garden. If I was a betting man, I would guess this was the owner of the bungalow. He was having a right old wobbler. He insisted his furniture was put back in the house, right now. Dale informed him that his men's health was a priority, not the ruined furniture. The owner then informed Dale that his men, meaning us, were to clean it and get it under cover. Dale clenched his teeth and his fists, told the irate owner that was not going to happen, and that he was to complain to whoever he needed to, with regards to the Argentines vandalising his property. Jamie turned and looked at me, with a rarely-seen worried look on his face. Would Dale forget himself and his position, and just wade into the civvy? Place your bets. The argument then turned onto the subject of who gave us permission to stay in his house. This was just getting better by the minute. I'm not an aggressive person at the best of times, but I now wanted

Dale to lose his cool, and smash this civvy prick all over the garden. Disappointingly, Dale was not taking the bait. He calmly informed this prick that he was to air his displeasure to the Brigade Liaison Officer, who was stationed with Brigade Headquarters at Government House. With that, the civvy stormed off, probably towards Brigade, and as he marched off, he was ranting on about how we should hurry up and go home. What a wanker. Dale slowly turned on his heels, and found Justin stood on the porch, nursing a brew and a beaming smile. Dale vented. "These fucking people."

Justin chuckled. "I've made you a tea, Sergeant Major. I was worried you'd beat him up, but well done for not doing so."

Dale looked at the tea for a second, and then accepted it. Justin and Phil patted him on the shoulder, and went back inside. Dale took a sip, when suddenly his eyes narrowed to a glare. "What are you pair of idiots looking at?" He was talking to us. Jamie and I looked at each other for inspiration, caught bang to rights. "Piss off," he told us, "before I feel the urge to have this furniture cleaned." He emphasised the piled-up chairs with a kick. We skirted past him and went into the bungalow, trying not to laugh.

Personally, I'd passed the point of giving a shit about these backward farming fuckwits. The Argies were more than welcome to the place, if this was what the people were like. We hadn't ventured any further into town as of yet, so hopefully, the two bell-ends we'd met at this stage were a minority. The remainder of the evening passed without much going on, apart from smoking, chatting, and listening to really long guitar instrumentals from a grown man in a school uniform. And before you ask, it wasn't one of the lads.

CHAPTER 15: The Service

The following morning was a slow and lazy affair. We were not due to have our church service in town until late morning, so there was no need for a mad rush to the shaving queue. I lay in my bag, just watching the world go by. The majority of the lads who had the shits yesterday had a bit of colour back in their cheeks, and were now back in the land of the living. Some of the early birds were up and dressed already, sorting out their Bergens. Some smoked, just outside the front door. The conversations were a random collection of subjects you would eavesdrop on in a pub; the due date of a baby, the price of a patio in Andover, their dickhead neighbours' D.I.Y in the middle of the night, stuff like that. Jamie was still nothing more than a sleeping green maggot next to me.

Word came round for the church service. Only one magazine would be carried, attached to rifles, but Gimpy gunners would not have belts fitted, and we were to leave all our kit at the bungalow. We were to be in berets and combats, nothing more. The majority of the room were still in bed, so I didn't feel the need to turf my arse out of bed, anytime soon. My theory was short lived, when Dale walked in from outside, and told us all to get up and get sorted. It took a brave man to ignore Dale, when there was stuff he wanted doing. Green maggots soon came to life.

267

Jamie sat up, with the hood still up on his bag. "You can do breakfast, I can't be arsed."

I clambered out of my bag, and slowly got dressed. Once shaved and boots polished, I rummaged through mine and Jamie's Bergens for food, and got to work in the garden with cooking. Just to keep the cold off, I had the duvet jacket on, which still smelt a bit ropey.

Jamie joined me outside, now dressed, but looking not too sprightly. "I had a terrible dream last night," he said.

"Oh yeah," I replied, "what about?"

"I dreamt we had to get out of these houses and move back onto Longdon, until it was time to get on the boat. Everything was frozen."

"Blimey, that's a bit random."

It would be the start of a long spell of random fucked up dreams for Jamie, nothing to do with combat, just a random collection of images all thrown together, as he would put it. We ate breakfast with not much to chatter about. We were rather bored of sitting in Stanley already. The worst bit was not knowing when we could go home.

Breakfast finished, and we went about making sure our shit was sorted for the church service. When the time came, Dale called the Company out of their bungalows onto the road. We gathered on the road, and got into three ranks facing the centre of Stanley, as if we were going to march onto a parade. Sergeants and above formed up at the rear of the Company. Dale ordered us to walk casually down the road, and then wait for the other companies in the Battalion to join us.

After a bit of milling about, with everyone trying to be in charge, the Battalion was finally in three ranks, ready to march to church. For those it applied to, rifles were to be tucked in under the right armpit, and Gimpys were to be carried on the right shoulder. OB moved into a position where he could command the Battalion. He roared out the order for attention. The locals who came out to line the street got a bit of a fright. He gave us the order to quick march, and the Battalion set off, all in step into town. As we began to march, all the locals lining the street cheered and waved us on. It came as a relief, since the first couple we'd met had really got our backs up, and we pretty much tarnished them all with the same brush. I was so happy we were wrong. I felt myself swelling with pride, and I must admit I was enjoying this march to church. As the Battalion drew up alongside the church, OB roared at us to halt, and we crashed to a standstill. The Commanding Officer and company commanders were already waiting for us at the front of the church, chatting with the locals and the media. OB ordered one rank at a time to file into the church. It took a bit of time, but the entire Battalion plus some locals and media managed to squeeze into the little church for our service.

The Battalion's padre, Fran, was what you could confidently call one of the few conscripts in the British Army. A man of the cloth, let it be said, but vicars tend to be pressed into a couple of years' military service, so they can be the spiritual anchor for young men who have to destroy fellow man as a profession. Padres assumed the rank of captain, just to add weight to their role in a unit, but they rarely threw their weight around, with regards to what we call rock, paper and rank. Fran was a scouser, I met him when I first joined the Battalion, since as part of the induction into the unit, you had to attend padre hour, so you knew you had an impartial shoulder to cry on, if you felt the chain of command couldn't help. Padre hour was a laugh. He cracked jokes, and even when he was trying to be serious, you'd roll up laughing because his strong scouse accent made it sound like stand-up comedy. He was hard as woodpecker's lips before he joined the church. He was a bouncer and bare knuckle fighter, and had the scars on his face and knuckles to prove it. His tattoos were as good as any Para's, let me tell you.

Fran asked for us to remove our berets, and then commenced the service. He reflected on the entire campaign as a whole. San Carlos, the lunacy of the Argentine pilots. The horrible march east. He then was very detailed and sincere about Mount Longdon; our casualties, friends and enemy. He asked for a moment of silence, and began to read out the names of those that had fallen. You could hear a pin drop in that church. When he read out the names of Danny, Tony, Kyle, Brandon and John, I swallowed hard to avoid the lump in my throat, but my eyes welled up, and I could only just about hold it together. I peered left and right of me. Hard men were openly sobbing, sniffing heavily. Arms went around friends' shoulders, backs were rubbed, and there was no shame in crying. We had been through one hell of a time in the last few weeks, and the whole magnitude of what we had undertaken now caught up with us. Once all the names were read out, Fran stood silent for reflection. His eyes were now glazed and bloodshot. One of his grim duties was to formally identify the soldiers, when their bodies were back-loaded to Teal, prior to them going into a temporary grave. This was his Battalion and his war, and his parish that were now dead, after dying and being maimed on that cold grim mountain.

He asked us to replace our berets, and thanked us for coming. OB stood up at the front, and asked us to leave in an orderly fashion, but told us to feel free to have a look around Port Stanley at our leisure, returning to our Company lines when ready. This was, as far as wars were concerned, an afternoon off.

We slowly moved outside, and there were small groups of lads, wandering off in all directions. Jamie and I decided to wander along the beach road, just to have a look about. There were prisoners mooching about with brooms and black bin liners, picking up random rubbish from the gutter, whilst their guards looked on. Our Second Battalion were yet to have their church service, and were cracking on with clear-up duties. We nodded to the guards, and continued on our way. Along the sea front, the wind had really picked up, and really bit through my clothing. I had a shirt, woollen jersey and my smock on, but no duvet jacket. I felt it bad taste to wear it, considering where we had just been. Besides, I didn't want Dale or OB catching me with it on, since that would be grief I just didn't need. As we walked past a gap in the bungalows, we noticed a huge trailer with what looked like four long light-grey crates. One of them had an end missing, and they were all angled upwards at nearly forty five degrees. What the hell were they? I peered in the end of the open crate, and it appeared to be all scorched and burnt inside. The crates were made of a metal of some kind, and had French writing in a black font. Jamie and I were none the wiser.

"I wouldn't prat around with that, if I was you," said a voice. We peered around the other side of the crates, and there stood a couple of military police.

Jamie stroked the cased end of one of the crates. "What is it?"

"Exocet," answered one of them, "anti-ship missile."

So that was the streak of light we saw shoot out of Stanley that night. "Fucking hell," I said, shaking my head. French missiles in Argentine hands, I thought a couple of high-profile heads might roll for this one.

Jamie and I continued with our sightseeing. We just wandered down whatever street looked inviting. Some were ransacked, with military kit all over the place. Down one particular street was a column of armoured cars, about ten of them. We walked around them with interest, thanking our lucky stars that these bad boys were not deployed. They looked brand new, probably taken off a ship, parked up here and forgotten about. Up and down the street, the locals just went about their business, some saying hello as they passed. In a children's playground next to the swings was one of the biggest artillery pieces I had ever seen. It wasn't ready for action, still in its stowed position. If they had got this beast into the fight, they could have really given us a pasting on that mountain. If the Argentines had been aware of what hardware they had at their disposal, and had the cunning and knowhow to use it effectively, we could very well be sitting up in the mountains even now, freezing our arses off, running low on ammo, scary shit.

Stanley wasn't the biggest town in the world, and it wasn't long before we'd seen pretty much all it had to offer. Prisoners were clearing up their mess all over the town, all looking very miserable and bloody cold. We thought of taking a look at the airport, but I couldn't be arsed to go and look at a shot-up airfield, occupied by a miserable army.

CHAPTER 16: The Canberra and the Norland

When Jamie and I arrived back at the bungalow, most of the platoon had already been there a while, and were in their usual positions. We got ourselves a brew on the go, when Davo walked in and called for everyone's attention. "Listen up, guys, I have some news you might be interested in. The OC and Dale have flown to Teal, for a small service for our boys. The prisoners will be shipped home on the Canberra, starting tomorrow." If he was expecting cheers, they weren't forthcoming. Fuck them, when are we going home? "Once the prisoners are out of here, we will hand in all our ammo and specialist kit to Phil, who will be getting it ready to freight on the Norland." This was more like it. "Once the ship is packed, we will board it along with the Second Battalion, getting the fuck out of here."

There was a thunderous roar from the lads. This was sweet music to our ears; getting the fuck out of here, going home, amazing. Almost straightaway, AC/DC crashed into life. Hairs on the back of my neck stood on end. GI's on their way home from Vietnam must have had this feeling flowing through them, knowing there was an end to their ordeal. Still floating on the good news, I went outside and savoured my brew in the cold sunshine.

Some of the lads went about packing their Bergens, as if we were about to get on the boat, right now. They were almost like children on Christmas Eve, wishing tomorrow would hurry up. It would all come soon enough, and we could hopefully catch some of the British summer, which would be a damn sight warmer than this one. I went to bed that night, without a snowball's chance in hell of sleeping, since the room was just a beehive of conversation, and packing of personal gear.

Morning came, the same as the last couple. Piss, wash, shave, get dressed, tea, coffee, nicotine for those that required it, and the same bland breakfast. There was however a very beautiful sight sat out in the harbour, for us to look at whilst we ate. As I emerged from the bungalow, I could see some of the Company gathered on the beach, admiring the view. I strolled down to join them, and sure as shit, there she was, in all her white, rusty and bullet-holed glory, the Canberra. Landing craft were ferrying the first batches of prisoners from shore to ship, and slowly but surely filling the boat. She was too big, and sat too deep in the water to be able to moor up at the jetty, hence the landing craft. It would take a fucking age to fill her with the thousands of prisoners that were queuing from the jetty, all the way back towards the airport. I don't think we complained too much, we were just glad to see her. Fuck knows how long it would take for her to sail to Argentina, off-load and steam back. It didn't matter; we would soon be out of there.

We milled about for the remainder of the day, with the Canberra slowly filling. Phil made the command decision to start receiving specialist equipment from the guys, such as night sights, binoculars, compasses, even watches from those that had to be issued one, mainly commanders. The ammo would be a mission for tomorrow. It took next to no time to gather all the kit required off the guys, and we all lent Phil a hand, getting his freight ready to go for loading onto the Norland, whenever she would arrive. The loading of prisoners lasted well into the night, but the view was just as marvellous, since the Canberra's lights were on. In the dark, she looked even bigger.

The following morning, the Canberra set sail, and it appeared the Argentine Army had as good as vanished. Stanley was a ghost town. Even the locals were treating themselves to a lie in. Word came around for the Battalion to get its freight down to the jetty, ready for the Norland's arrival. Second Battalion would load theirs first, followed by us. Judging by the time it took us to load all our shit onto the Canberra in Southampton back in April, we knew there was no rush to get down there, so we got all our ammo packed up.

Phil instructed the Company to get all their ammo to the beach. Word came down from the quartermaster of the Battalion that any ammo broken out of its packaging would be gathered up and destroyed. Another small African nation's budget was about to become fish food. Apart from the crates of ammo we'd got off the Chinook a few days ago, nothing else could be salvaged. The guys, including me, had our ammo piled up in front of us, and as Phil came down the line to confirm what could be saved, a very scary revelation became clear. Almost all of the Company were in possession of Argentine ammunition. Our ammo was one tracer, with every three normal on a belt. The Argentines had a mixed bag of orange and green tracer, on a belt of normal rounds. The green tracer was in fact armour-piercing rounds, holy shit. It quickly became apparent that we had run out of our own ammo quicker than planned, and had resorted to scrounging ammo from enemy positions, some food for thought maybe, for the big planners of this whole bloody campaign. A landing craft was arranged, for engineers to take the ammo away and feed the fish with it.

Early afternoon, the MV Norland made an appearance in the harbour. Second Battalion were on the jetty with all their freight ready to go, and the manpower to get it on in a short amount of time. We had begun to get our shit to the waterfront, with whatever was to hand. We had managed to scrounge captured trucks, tractors and trailers, you name it. Our Company freight was pretty poxy, compared to the likes of Support Company. They had mortars, machineguns and MILAN to get freighted onto the ship, and that took a shitload of muscle and sweat. B Company patiently waited its turn. The Battalion's ammo that was still crated from San Carlos was a bastard of a job, and all hands to the pump were needed to get that cracked. It was almost dark when it was our turn to get our freight onboard, but when you know that the end is upon you, you don't mind busting a gut through the night.

We returned to the bungalow in the early hours of the following morning, all giddy with excitement of our impending departure. I packed all that was not needed tomorrow, so there would be minimal fucking about. No one slept. We just sat around shooting the shit, smoking, laughing, drinking brews, all the usual carry-on of troops just burning time.

The early light of dawn arrived, so we got our shit together, and moved it out of the bungalow into the garden. Davo spammed me with wiping down the kitchen and mopping the floor, wanting to leave the place in as good a state as possible, despite the shitty furniture still stacked in the garden. Everyone mucked in getting the bungalow shipshape.

We closed the front door behind us. It was very cold outside, our breath very prominent in the cold air, but we didn't mind, the air felt good for the first time in a while. Dale shouted for us to get our gear on, and form up onto the road. I put my gear on with ease, since we no longer had loads of ammo, water and rations rammed in it.

Once the Company had finished larking about, we managed to get into three ranks. Dale didn't bellow drill commands, he just told us to start walking. We knew where to go. The other companies were marching parallel to us in the next street. They were all smiles as well, and laughter could be heard, until one of their seniors told them to keep the noise down.

We arrived at the waterfront. Without being told, most of the Company were removing Bergens and sitting on them. Some stood and lit cigarettes. We just passed the time of day once again, waiting to be called forward to board the ship. The Norland was half the size of the Canberra, and she was moored at the jetty, which suited us, no more bloody landing craft. It wasn't long before we received the order we had dreamed of for the last couple of days. We got to our feet and put our gear back on. As B Company began to climb the gangplank, I got all emotional, but managed to get a grip of myself, before I became a sobbing mess. With glazed eyes, I looked up at the Norland, whose decks towered above me, and instantly I was overcome with the desire for a nice long hot shower and a beer. The shower would come soon enough, my first in weeks.

   As for the beer, that would have to officially wait until I was eighteen.

EPILOGUE: Return to Mount Longdon

We arrived at RAF Mount Pleasant after a bloody long flight, nineteen hours. That didn't include the three hour refuel at Ascension Island. The DC-10 was on its regular shuttle from Birmingham, all the way down to East Falkland. Jamie leaned across me, peered out of the window and nodded. "Yep," he said, "same shite weather."

When we were allowed to leave the aircraft, we made our way down the steps, and followed a member of the RAF movements control people into the terminal. Mount Pleasant wasn't exactly Heathrow, but it was a busy airport nonetheless. Whilst waiting for our baggage to be recovered from the plane, we had to listen to a mandatory briefing about minefield awareness. The place was still littered with the fuckers. We each got issued a map, highlighting the areas that were out of bounds, yet civilian organisations were working tirelessly, searching the open moorland with a fine tooth comb for the little bastards. It was common for cattle to wander where they shouldn't, and the farmer would hear a loud thud, as his prized Hereford would cripple itself. Once the brief was finished, our luggage was on the carousel, and it wasn't long before we claimed what was ours.

Our guide for the visit was a rather attractive redheaded woman called Vicky, who ushered our group outside to a series of Land Rovers. We all clambered in and slowly made our way out of the airbase, en route to Port Stanley. A solid hard-standing road had long since been built, connecting all the settlements to the capital.

Our party consisted of me, Jamie, Davo and Phil. We were accompanied by mine and Jamie's sons, Robert and Daniel respectively. Both Robert and Daniel were corporals in our old Battalion, and were veterans of both Iraq and Afghanistan. My boy Robert was in B Company. Daniel was a member of Patrols, who still carried out the same tasks as they did thirty years ago. Without sounding biased, they were both good operators, and had the humility to ask their superiors if they were unsure of things. They both volunteered to come with us all the way here during their leave, since the Battalion was once again getting ready for Helmand province, and couldn't spare them at any other time, much to the dismay of their girlfriends.

I had recently retired from the Army in the rank of Major. My last appointment in the Battalion was quartermaster, which was not at all fun, the entire Battalion equipment list and budget on my shoulders. Be too lavish with the equipment and the money, you got your hand slapped by the Whitehall bean counters. Be too cautious, and the boys on the shop floor thought you were a career-minded wanker, so you couldn't win.

Now, in my free time, I walked the dog, kept myself in pretty decent shape, enjoyed a handsome pension, and whatever hobbies I had going on. I tried golf, but that was just too boring for me. I'd rather watch paint dry.

Jamie left the Army a few years before me, finishing his time with the Battalion as the Regimental Sergeant Major. Who the hell let that clown be RSM wants their head seeing to. But my best friend did a great job. All the way through our careers and lives, we had been thick as thieves. He just had enough at the end of his twenty-two year career, and had the bottle to leave. He got involved with the security scene over in Iraq for a short time, but when he found out it was full of Walter Mitty clowns, who only talked a good gunfight, he told them to poke it up their arses, and returned to the UK to become a personal trainer. He now owns his own gym, and enjoys a very comfortable life.

Davo married Sam when he got back. They now live in Chichester, couple of kids that have now pissed off to university still costing him a fortune. He left the Army as a captain, after serving as a company commander at our recruit depot. He now does adventure hikes and stuff, with civilian clients paying him a fortune to take them up Snowdon and places like that. Sam works with him and squares away all his admin, whilst he walks his party all over the hills. Not a bad living.

Phil, our old Company quartermaster, was the eldest in our party. He retired after a full career, and went on to be a Yeoman Warder of all things. Taking crazy tourists all around the Tower of London, telling them all the grim stories, in which they hung on his every word. Phil and his wife lived in apartments in the Tower, and I was invited to spend the weekends there on a number of occasions. Drinking in their exclusive bar was a nice experience, listening to all their stories of this and that, and not having to tell them the same stories over and over again, like when you first meet people and they find out you were in the Army.

The drive to Port Stanley took about forty minutes, and it wasn't long before the road took you around the base of Mount Harriet, on our left side. Mount Harriet was one of the commando objectives on the same night as Longdon. As we got closer to Stanley, Sapper Hill and Mount William could clearly be seen over to our left, with the summit of Tumbledown further to the north. We entered the outskirts of Stanley, and were stunned with how much it had grown.

There were building projects all over the shop. A lot of money had really been poured into here. The islands had enjoyed the wealth of tourism since the war, as people became inquisitive about these small islands in the South Atlantic. We drove down to the waterfront where the jetty was, and that brought out a few memories. We took the mick out of Phil for that bloody long day, fucking around with the freight. He gave us the finger and just looked out the window, which made us roar even more. Back then, we wouldn't have dared make fun of Phil, since he was our Colour Sergeant, and we were just two cheeky Private soldiers. Our guide pulled up outside our dwellings. They would serve as home for the next few days. We clambered out, grabbing our gear, and made our way inside.

Vicky introduced us to the lady of the house, and she was in her early forties maybe, so therefore just a child when we were here last. She gave us the grand tour, and showed us to our rooms. Being typical soldiers, you never lose the habit; we literally slung our gear into our rooms and made our way back down to the little bar they had, and pitched up there for the rest of the evening. It was wonderful to be with my son and some old friends, chewing the fat and drinking beer. We put the world to rights with regards to our old Battalion, the rights and wrongs of Iraq and Afghanistan, and all the usual shit that pissed soldiers waffle on about, when they've had too many beers. The lady of the house was great company, and didn't mind staying up with us, while we put money behind her bar, and almost drunk the place dry. Our hangovers would not be forgiving in the morning.

What possessed me to drink that much was beyond me. Why do I do it? Like a dickhead, I had a hangover that would kill the average civilian, and had a long walk ahead of me today. I gingerly got out of bed, and got myself sorted. I would not be wearing uniform for this one. I had decent walking boots and cargo trousers, with some decent warm clothing, and the type of windproof jacket that is all the rage in the mountaineering community. I had my walking rucksack, which had some items that I needed to deliver, whilst I was here.

I made my way downstairs to breakfast, and took no prisoners on the menu. I ordered a Full Monty truckers' special, with extra fried bread. I was going to need it today. One by one, the survivors of last night emerged, and joined me at the table. Robert and Daniel were the last to appear, saying something about how the old and bold can put their drink away. I caught Phil's gaze and he just winked. He then stated that the Battalion couldn't drink for shit these days, since they spent too much time in the gym, and worrying about looking pretty. This made Jamie and I chuckle, and our sons held up their hands in capitulation.

Once we'd eaten ourselves back into the land of the living, and drank our bodyweight in tea, our very enthusiastic guide arrived. She was mainly there to help Phil, since we'd elected to walk, but Phil's TABbing days were long over, and he and the sexy redhead were going to meet us at the top.

We got our gear together, and made our way outside. Phil and Vicky clambered into the Rover, and drove out of town. We began our trek at a gentle stroll. The weather forecast was set to be good for this time of year. It would remain cold, but nothing we couldn't handle. We kept to the road that followed the beach. We came across the South Atlantic memorial, which we took time to look at and read. We then continued on, to where our bungalow was situated. It was still there. The garden had received a makeover, but other than that, the bungalow was still as it was, just with a new lick of paint. No one was in, but a neighbour called out of their window, stating that the owners were back in the UK visiting family. We thanked them for the information and pressed on. We were on the road that would lead us to Moody Brook Barracks and the base of Wireless Ridge. On our left side around the racecourse were a load of new buildings, something to do with a cable and wireless company. We eventually arrived at the old barracks site. The barracks had long since been ripped down, replaced by a cluster of official looking buildings. I remember watching some of our lads searching a couple of prisoners here, giving them a cigarette, and sending them on their way.

We began our ascent of Wireless Ridge. Luckily, the three of us old bastards were still in semi-decent shape, with Rob and Dan streaking off and waiting for us at the top, fresh as daisies. So they bloody well should, they were serving members of the Parachute Regiment, something seriously wrong if they were lagging behind us. We got to the top and caught our breath, before we made our way over to the memorial that was for our Second Battalion. It was a large silver cross, with numerous wreaths around the base of it. Three names were engraved there, the guys they lost on that night. It caused me to reflect. This was meant to be one of our objectives, and these guys had already done their bit at Goose Green, such a shame. I took off my rucksack and reached into it. I fished out a large bottle of single malt, and placed it next to the guys' plaque. No one said a word, it wasn't needed.

I got my gear back on, and turned around. And there it was. I remember as a Sergeant Major, having to attend a veterans' lunch at the old Airborne Forces Museum in

Aldershot. It was located in the old barracks, which were once our recruit depot. That place was nothing more than a compound of misery and suffering for me as a recruit, and as a Sergeant Major on that particular day, I was overwhelmed with butterflies and dread, that's how much I detested that place. Career-wise, I almost shot myself in the foot, when I refused to go there as an instructor, where it would be me dishing out the torment. I just couldn't bring myself to go there. The same could be said in the case of what I was looking at now. From where I was stood, Longdon looked like a sleeping dinosaur, with us stood on its tail.

The plan was to meet Phil and Vicky at the site of our RAP, and climb up to the memorial as a group. We began our ascent of Longdon at a casual pace, since I was keen to have a real good nose around. We came off the high ground of Wireless onto the shallow saddle that separated the two features, and we began to climb up onto A Company's end-battle position on the summit, known as Full Back. The cover they would have had during the shelling appeared rather sparse, we definitely had the better cover that day. They were on a forward slope in full view of Stanley and the enemy gun line on the racecourse, not ideal at all.

We inspected the bunkers. Those with overhead protection had through time and bad weather partially collapsed, revealing the contents within. Rotten sleeping bags, a mouldy kit bag with some clothing spilling out of it, empty bullet cases, old ration tins well-faded over the years. Some of the old trenches we found had no cover, and were now overgrown with heath grass and ferns.

In the centre of A Company's position was the remnants of a flak gun, its chassis all rusted and buckled out of shape, and around it was the random debris of equipment we couldn't recognise. I stood behind it, and noticed it had a fantastic arc of fire, all the way up to our position on Fly Half. Was this the nemesis that kept 4 Platoon pinned in the alleys? The history books would have you believe it was naval gunfire that knocked it out, but after a number of chats with members of Support Company on the way home, they claimed the crew was obliterated by machinegun fire, and the weapon knocked out by MILAN. I didn't see what happened that night, so this claim will remain out with the jury.

We slowly made our way up to Fly Half. It became apparent how open the top of Longdon was, and it would be plain suicide for anyone to want to occupy it, since it was a forward-facing slope towards Stanley, dominated by Tumbledown to the south, hence the reason that the

Battalion hunkered down on the north side, throughout our time on the objective. Over to our left side was the infamous anti-tank gun that knocked out one of our support teams. It now faced Tumbledown, which I found rather bizarre. Why would anyone move it? As we climbed up further, we found evidence of where the fire-support teams had once been. Spent cases and machinegun link all over the place, rusty broken ammo tins littered everywhere. Those teams were truly exposed that night, with just darkness as cover; it took some guts to remain in that position, for all of that time.

 We moved over to our right, and came to the lip of the bowl. How different it looked after three decades. Some of the bunkers could still be seen, the rest were overgrown with ferns and heath grass. We carefully clambered down into the bowl. Amongst the ferns, I tripped on an empty twisted ammo tin, and found the odd rifle magazine, rusted beyond use. We inspected a couple of the bunkers. Pretty much the same contents as encountered on Full Back. The grim corpses and vile smell were long gone. We made our way down to the bottom of the bowl, and moved around to the left. Phil and Vicky's Rover came into view, marking the old RAP site. Vicky knew the spot well, since this is where she would start the Longdon battlefield trip for the tourists, which I found rather bizarre. I never would have classed

Mount Longdon as a site for tourism, but the general public have a morbid fascination for human conflict, me included.

We walked down to the vehicle. As we drew close, they both got out. Phil got himself ready for the short sharp climb to the top. Vicky suggested she remained with the vehicle, since she wisely felt her knowledge of the battle wasn't required today. We thanked her for her understanding, and arranged to meet her in a couple of hours at the RAP site.

We set off with Phil, making our way towards our old start line. We kept to his pace, and every now and again we stopped to recollect what had been happening, at a certain point in time during the battle. Back then, when I was freezing cold and fucking scared, I never imagined myself walking the battlefield with friends, going over the events of that awful night, all that time ago.

We began to skirt around to our left, and climb up toward the alleys. It looked so much more of a placid place this time around, not the grim deadly objective that chewed up 4 Platoon that night. Because Phil was not as young as he once was, we didn't plan to climb up through the alleys to get back to the summit.

Rob and Dan became truly fascinated with the whole experience. They also added a modern-day view of how they felt today's Battalion would have dealt with the objective. We all stood facing our old start line, with Patrols expert Daniel showing us the route he would have taken, if he was guiding us in. To be fair, he wasn't far off the actual route we took.

We turned and faced up on to 5 Platoon's objective, their route up to Fly Half. It was a real maze of rock, long heath grass and ferns. The wooden beams of a few of the positions that had overhead cover could be seen, but time and weather had perished a lot of the bunker features.

I took the opportunity to show Rob and Dan the bunker I fell into, its wooden supports now badly rotted, the hole now waterlogged. My boy put a hand on my shoulder, thanking me for winning the brawl that night, and gave me a hug, the silly sod.

We began to pick our way up through the rocks and long grass, inspecting the bunkers as we went. It wasn't long before we found Danny's bunker. It was no less John or Brandon's, don't get me wrong, but I always referred to it as Danny's. As Davo, Jamie and I explained what happened here, our boys shook their heads and let out a low whistle. It was at this point Phil apologised for not being with the Company that night, and got a bit silly and emotional. In all honesty, it wasn't his job. His job was to get ammo, rations and water forward, and he'd passed any fighting appointments in his career by that point. He composed himself, and apologised for being a silly old sod.

We climbed up onto Fly Half, and made our way over to the left, where the Battalion memorial stood. As with Wireless Ridge, there stood a large silver cross. At its base was a large collection of plaques dedicated to the Battalion, plus plaques dedicated to individuals by both family and friends, who had made the long pilgrimage here. We took our time reading them, reflecting on every name that was engraved. I removed my rucksack, and carefully placed it at my feet, unzipping the main compartment. Carefully, I removed a small wreath, which was dedicated to the Battalion by Dale's widow. Dale had lost his long struggle with cancer just last year, and had never returned to Longdon. Dale was regarded as a legend amongst the old B Company boys, and across the Battalion as a whole. We all missed him. He acted more like your dad than the Company Sergeant Major, which kept the boys in line on more than one occasion. He was without a doubt a true role model of mine. All the way through my career, I just wanted to do right by him, and do things his way. And it bloody worked. I missed him.

I placed the wreath at the base of the cross, and dug into the rucksack once again. I pulled out a large bottle of single malt for the boys, placing it next to the wreath. Davo had found a large ammo tin, which had a visitors' book in it. The book was in a thick, clear plastic bag for obvious reasons. We all added our thoughts and messages of respect into the book, and ensured it was well wrapped up, back in the tin for the next visitors.

I had one more gift to deliver. I pulled from the rucksack the duvet jacket Jamie had got for me in the RAP. It had been laundered a thousand times since, and had been my chosen piece of warm kit, throughout my career. It had given me an element of kudos. I was that bloke who had a dead Argentine's jacket. Whether I was in barracks, or away on a career course, the jacket was the topic of conversation. I lost count how many times Rob had asked for the jacket, but I had always refused to let him take it. I placed it at the base of the memorial, and found a large enough rock to hold it in place, so it wouldn't blow away.

I didn't need it anymore.

Mount Longdon

This name broke the hearts of many mothers on that awful night.

Thirty years ago.

Their sons are listed here.

JUAN DOMINGO BALDINI
VICTOR RODRIGUEZ

IAN MCKAY
ALFREDO GATTINI

DARIO ROLANDO RIOS
IAN SCRIVENS

TONY GREENWOOD
GUILLERMO GRANADO

PEDRO ALBERTO OROZCO
DONATO GRAMISCI

TIMOTHY JENKINS
JOSE LUIS DEL HIERRO

MARCELO MASSAD
GERALD BULL

SCOTTY WILSON
ISSAC ERASMO ROCHA

JOSE LUIS RODRIGUEZ
OMAR ANIBAL BRITO

STEVE HOPE
MACEDONIO RODRIGUEZ

RICARDO HERRERA
DAVID SCOTT

STUART MCLAUGHLIN
MIGUEL ARRASCAETA

PEDRO VOSKOVIC
JAMES MURDOCH

STEWART LAING
NESTOR GONZALEZ

CARLO A HORNOS
RICHARD ABSOLON

PHILIP WEST
MIGUEL GONZALEZ

MANUEL A ZELARAYAN
CHRIS LOVETT

PETER HIGGS
JULIO HECTOR MAIDANA

ALEJANDRO VARGAS
CRAIG JONES

PETER HEDICKER
LUIS ALBERTO DIAZ

ROLANDO PACHOLCZUK
ALEX SHAW

NEIL GROSE
DANTE LUIS PEREYRA

MANUEL JUAREZ
JASON BURT

KEITH MCCARTHY
ANGEL BENITEZ

RAMON QUINTANA
ENRIQUE RONCONI

MARK DODSWORTH
ALBERTO PETRUCELLI

MIGUEL FALCON
MIGUEL ANGEL PASCUAL

JOHN CROW
JULIO ROMERO

SERGIO CARBALLIDO
ELBIO EDUARDO ARAUJO

ALL WARS ARE CIVIL WARS, BECAUSE ALL MEN ARE BROTHERS

-

Francois Fenelon